# THE JOY ROBBERS

## Cyvette Guerra

impact
books

Library of Congress Catalogue Number: 78-66871

Hardback
ISBN 0-914850-05-9
MO579

Paperback
ISBN 0-914850-39-3
MO575

First Edition

# DEDICATION

To my sons, Travis, Thad, and Bobby John as an expression of gratitude for their steady growth deeper into the heart of Christ.

To their father and my husband, Gene, for his steadfast dedication to Christ. He is a living example to us.

To my mom and dad, John and Lyvonne Flowers, for their unending love that has undergirded our family.

# ACKNOWLEDGMENTS

I want to acknowledge gratefully those people who have made this work possible.

. . . my husband, Gene, who was available when I needed a scriptural sounding board.

. . . my close friends, Diane Hunt, Joe Brown, and his wife, Connie, for their unflagging dedication to the rewrite. Together we burned the midnight oil preparing the manuscript for "send-off."

. . . Emma Cox for her excellent typing assistance and encouragement.

. . . Ann Severance, editor of Impact Books, a hats off, standing ovation for a job well done!

Finally, a big thank you to all the other wonderful people at The Benson Company who made me a part of their family.

# CONTENTS

# INTRODUCTION

"Smile—God loves you!" is a familiar slogan appearing on bumper stickers, lapel buttons, and highway billboards.

The fact is, there aren't as many smiling Christians as there should be. It seems there is always some problem, some situation, some obstacle that looms in the background, keeping us from experiencing true joy. Just when the horizon begins to dawn with the hope of victory, some unexpected setback comes along that sends us into a tailspin of defeat! It reminds us of many weather forecasts—sunshine is promised but all we get is rain!

When I first accepted Christ, I wondered if possibly someone had overstated what I was to experience as a result of that acceptance. I was promised love, joy, peace, patience, kindness, self-control, but little of that became an instant reality. It was as if someone had sugarcoated this thing called Christianity, saying, "Take a believer pill and all your troubles will vanish—no more worries, no more heartaches. The Jesus way is a sure cure for financial problems, marital strife, and the generation gap." If only that had been true! Many times I was more confused than before becoming a Christian!

This lack of understanding about the nature of being born again causes many new Christians to ask themselves, "Why am I not happy?" "Why do I get so discouraged?" "Why hasn't joy become a reality in my life?"

Ask, and ye shall receive, that your joy may be full (John 16:24).

Good news! The joy will come. These words of Jesus promise it. The problems will not disappear, but the joy will come. I have discovered through many dark hours that victory is waiting to be claimed by every believer. How? By applying some principles clearly outlined in God's Word. I long to share with you some of those principles that have come alive for me. Through a better understanding of God's Word, I have found the joy Jesus promised to all believers! You can discover it too!

Joy is often confused with simple pleasure. The joy of which the Bible speaks fills one from the inside out. In other words it doesn't begin with the facial muscles but the heart muscle, causing us to smile from within. We can be joyful and content **inwardly** in spite of outward circumstances. We come to experience an inner peace and tranquility because of our deep-rooted belief in God's ability to provide. Then, even through our tears, we can say, "I know all things work together for **good** to them that love God" (Rom. 8:28).

What, then, are joy robbers? They are subtle intruders that enter our lives through unlocked doors of human weakness and convince us that Christianity is a hoax. They can undermine our faith. They can steal the joy of our salvation. Our goal will be to unmask and expose their true identity.

Before you get the wrong impression, I want you to know that I don't "fly high" all the time. I still have problems that seem bigger than I, but I have learned that none of those problems are bigger than God. For that reason the joy of which I speak is so deep, so firmly grounded, so secure that nothing can take it from me.

While on vacation in Florida recently, our family visited a small zoo in Sanford. As we walked across a little wooden bridge spanning a lazy brook, we noticed two hawks perched on a dead tree stump. They were beautiful against the natural setting of the woods. As we were wondering how the zoo keeper had managed to train the birds to stay within the confines of the zoo, one unfolded his wings and began to ascend gracefully. No sooner had he become airborne than he was rudely snatched back to his perch by a thin leather strap attached to his leg. Our mouths flew open in shock as the beauty of the moment became a mockery! That magnificent bird fluttered and flapped his powerful wings struggling to be free until he surrendered his efforts, resigning himself to the tyranny of the small leather strap. I wanted to cry. I longed to cut the bird loose so that he could experience the freedom for which he was born. Frustrated, I realized I did not have the authority to set that bird free. I knew all that was restraining him was an insignificant leather strap, yet I could not cut it.

The joy robbers are like that leather strap! Often they go unnoticed by the rest of the world. Sometimes we ourselves forget they are there until, like the hawk, we struggle to be free, only to feel ourselves snatched abruptly back to reality. But, thank God, this is where the analogy ends! We are the children of a Father whose truth can free us from the problems and circumstances that bind our hope and steal our joy.

> And ye shall know the truth, and the truth shall make you free (John 8:32).

His truth can release us to be all He created us to be. To that end we make this journey into the realm of the joy robbers.

# Part One
# The Joy Robbers

# Chapter 1

# Butterflies and Knee-Knockers
## (Fear)

In the past I've had the big "C" at least a hundred times. I've had cancer of the stomach, brain, abdomen, big toe, nose, pancreas, and at least ten malignant moles. Of course, no doctor was ever able to confirm my diagnosis, but I **knew** I was a walking miracle! After years of surviving all these diseases, it suddenly dawned on me that perhaps I was a little preoccupied with my body! One day I simply tired of taking my pulse and decided to turn my fear of ill health over to the Lord. Yes, the big "C" may sneak up on me, but frankly, I'd be grateful for the surprise! At least fear won't have robbed me of years of carefree joy in the Lord.

Ill health is only one thing in my life that has caused me to experience intense fear. While some of these fears were based on solid fact, others were simply figments of an overactive imagination. I do know one thing—those alarming feelings that activate the adrenalin glands and shift my heart into "high" come whether I've dreamed up the event or not. My mind can't tell the difference. I can literally scare myself to death! One of the wonderful things

God has done for me is to teach me how to deal with such fear.

Shortly after our second child was born, I experienced a series of anxiety attacks triggered by a blood-sugar imbalance. My blood sugar would fluctuate from high to a dangerous low in a matter of minutes, bringing on the anxiety. If you have never had an acute attack of anxiety, you cannot imagine what it is like.

The mind signals the body of impending danger. As if on cue, the heart begins to race. Hands sweat profusely and the mental state is one of irrational and uncontrollable fear. While you **know** there is no actual danger, you are powerless to convince your mind of that fact. Suddenly, you find yourself a prisoner to a body that has gone berserk.

Psychiatrists will tell you a human being cannot sustain a continued and prolonged attack. It was during this frightening experience that God began to teach me how to deal with fear. Much to my surprise, I discovered I did not have to remain at the mercy of my emotions.

Up until that time, I had geared my entire existence around avoiding anxiety, and that behavior naturally brought on more anxiety. These attacks literally controlled my life. They would so terrify me that I could not carry on the normal everyday activities of a wife and mother. It seemed there was no escape. My fear was so overwhelming that only God was big enough to deal with it.

Fear, I discovered, can also keep us from performing a God-given task. I remember a trip we took several years ago to Key West. Our mission, along with that of about twenty other people, was to undergird a church that was in spiritual trouble. We were to accomplish this by sharing our testimonies, leading discussion groups, and on the last day, participating in a commitment service led by our lay-witness leader.

Now the problem: The only way to reach Key West from St. Petersburg for a short weekend is by air. I was panic-stricken at the thought! I had not flown in years; and after my last flight, I had vowed I would never again set foot aboard another aircraft of any description!

We flew from St. Petersburg to Miami on a well-known airline. We all settled back into our cushioned seats as competent stewardesses offered us pillows, coffee, tea, or milk. The calm voice of the pilot kept us posted on our ascension and location. Everything was proceeding smoothly. I was quite proud of how readily I allowed God to calm my fears as I prayed for courage. Little did I know what lay ahead!

When we arrived in Miami, I discovered what everyone else already knew. There are only two commuter airlines that fly to Key West from Miami and both of them are very, very small. I got my first clue of how small as we walked toward the aircraft.

The plane, and I use the term loosely, was covered with grit and grease. Metallic rivets stood out loosely all over the fuselage. The aircraft was described to me by friends as a tail dragger. I thought it was broken, since the back part was so much lower than the front. It looked like a reject from World War II. As we approached the plane, the stewardess greeted us in a uniform that looked as though she had slept in it. She was **throwing** the luggage into the tail section of the plane.

By now there was no way to stop the flood of tears. My legs shook uncontrollably, making it even more difficult to maneuver to my seat.

Once aboard, a well-meaning friend said, "Don't worry, Cyvette, this plane has been flying for thirty years." That did it! I was sure thirty years was pushing it, and I decided God did not need **me** in Key West. I was making my exit. My husband looked at me as if he thought I was crazy. I told him he could pick me up on the way back, but I was **not** going to fly anywhere in that shoddy aircraft. I pointed to the screws coming out of the ceiling, the elastic in the magazine holders all stretched and torn, the air so hot it was difficult to breathe. Ignoring all these obvious defects, he politely grabbed me and plopped me back into my seat. I cried harder. He said I was going to fly to Key West whether God needed me or not because he refused to leave me in Miami alone. He then buckled me into my seat.

In desperation my thoughts turned to God and I cried inwardly, "God, help!" Just as quickly as I had formed the words, He answered, "Cyvette, it's my responsibility to see that this plane makes it safely to Key West, not yours."

I cannot tell you what a revelation that was to me. Instantly, I began to relax, confident that God was watching over me, plotting my destiny. I need not fear what could happen. I had done my part; I had managed to board the plane. God could not do that for me. With that step of faith, my responsibility ended and His began.

As the pilot and copilot approached the plane, now ready for takeoff, I noticed that they were not in uniform. They spoke broken English (Cuba, here we come!); but neither this fact nor their unprofessional appearance frightened me. The engines started and the plane began to vibrate violently as it headed down the runway. I was strangely unafraid. True to God's promise to me, we made it to Key West safely.

During the renewal weekend, I had the opportunity to share this spiritual discovery. At the ladies' luncheon on Saturday, a fellow team member sat beside me. As we were eating, she began to cry. When I asked her what was wrong, she confided that she had always had a terrible fear of speaking in front of people, yet she felt God wanted her to share what He was doing in her life. She knew the team leader was going to call on her after the luncheon, and she was scared to death! She also told me that, as she entered the building, she had asked God to seat her next to someone who could help her. How about that! God placed her next to someone who knew all about fear!

I began to relate my recent victory and told her what God had revealed to me. Then I said, "Carolyn, your only responsibility is to walk up to that podium. After that, it's up to God what happens. You will have done all you can do."

When we broke for the sharing time, Carolyn's name was called. She glanced at me tearfully and walked to the front. In a timid voice she said, "Before I begin, I want my new friend in Christ to pray for me." I prayed. Then Carolyn began to speak. Her testimony was deep and meaningful.

All of us fear something—whether it is flying, speaking in public, heights, or creepy, crawly things. Although one person's fears may seem insignificant or even laughable to another, they are nevertheless real and often incapacitating. There are some events, however, that inevitably produce fear for all

of us—those events with life-and-death consequences. Through such an experience with one of
our children, I learned how able God is.

After a weekend trip to Jacksonville Beach,
Florida, to visit grandparents, my family arrived
back home in St. Petersburg, exhausted! The
weekend, while enjoyable, was dampened by
sickness. I had developed a virus accompanied by
high fever, headache, a deep gagging cough, and
sore throat. I knew it would only be a matter of time
before the rest of the family caught the bug too. Our
ride home consisted of swallowing aspirin, sharing
germs, and settling arguments between understand-
ably cranky children.

By the time my husband, Gene, and I had settled
the boys in bed for the night, all three of them were
sick. I kept an especially close watch on Bobby
John, then only two, since he had  always run
unusually high fevers. I heard him cough and went in
to check on him. As I looked at him sleeping in his
crib, I was startled by the strange look on his face. He
had a fixed smile, unnaturally sweet, as if he were
dreaming. I reached down and picked him up. Instantly, I could feel the excessive heat generating
from his body. I laid him gently on the bahama bed
in his room so I could take his temperature. I un-
fastened a diaper pin, stuck it in the cushion, and
turned my eyes back to Bobby John's face just in
time to see his eyes roll back in his head. His body
began to convulse in small spasms as his hands
clenched into fists and his legs drew up to his abdomen. Horrified, I screamed for Gene. He grabbed
Bobby John and shook him, quickly dropping his
head toward the floor. Already he was turning blue.

Tom Burton, our next-door neighbor, was a
trained first-aid instructor and fireman. I raced

toward his house in my nightgown, not even stopping to grab a robe. Glancing back over my shoulder, I saw Gene in the hall with Bobby John high over his head. Gene was shaking him, and Bobby John was turning bluer by the second.

Tom's car was not in the driveway. My heart sank. It must be his twenty-four-hour shift at the fire station. I began to scream for his wife, Jenny, and her teenage sons, Mike and Jeff. I begged them to call a rescue squad or ambulance and hurry! Then I ran back to the house. Bobby John, now a deep ashen blue, was on the bathroom floor, his body jerking slightly. Gene was giving mouth-to-mouth resuscitation, moaning in futility between each breath. Bobby John's heart had stopped and no matter what he did, Gene could not force any air into his lungs. In desperation he ordered me to get him a razor blade. I knew he was going to attempt a tracheotomy. Since Bobby John was obviously dying, we had nothing to lose. I knew by the time the ambulance came it would be too late.

I ran to our bathroom in a wild panic. When I threw open the medicine cabinet, I literally could not see a thing! Everything was a blur! I felt Bobby John's life was in my hands, and I was powerless to help him. In great despair I cried out to the Lord. He descended like a dove. I know no other words to describe it. Instantly, His presence was everywhere. He was so real, I think I could have touched Him.

My eyes cleared quickly, and there before me lay a razor blade. It was as if God had been standing on the sidelines all along wanting to help and just waiting to be asked.

When I got back to Gene, Bobby John looked much worse. His body was now limp and motionless, his skin a sickening, deep blue. Death hovered nearby. Gene grabbed the blade from my hand and made a deep gash in Bobby John's throat. I gasped as the blade bit the tender tissue.

But I snapped back into action when Gene ordered me to find something to put in the trachea. Suddenly, I remembered an old enema bottle and tube in our closet. I began to fling clothes in all directions as I searched frantically. Travis, our oldest son, called out and I yelled at him to stay in bed, no matter what. Finding the tube, I raced back to Gene. Bobby John looked much the same, only now there was a trickle of blood oozing from the wound in his throat. I could hardly bear to listen to Gene's anguished groans in his desperate efforts to save our son. He made another deep cut into Bobby John's throat and inserted the tube.

At this point, Bobby John uttered a very faint gurgle. It was barely audible, yet a definite sign of hope. My spirits soared! Gene dropped everything and started the mouth-to-mouth resuscitation again. This time it worked! A miracle! Bobby John's color improved rapidly. His eyelids fluttered open and he smiled at Gene before his eyes rolled back into his head. "Fight, son, fight!" Gene pleaded.

In the meantime a police car pulled up in front of the house. I managed to tell the policeman what had happened. He radioed the ambulance and hospital to report the attempted tracheotomy, then hurried into the house to assist Gene. I didn't follow the policeman, but waited outside to be sure the ambulance found the right house.

I looked around and spotted my dear friend, Jenny, standing there shaking with fright and cold. Her boys were in the house trying to help Gene. Straining to hear the siren, I screamed at poor, shaking

Jenny to keep praying. Seconds later the ambulance screeched to a stop.

While the attendants rushed in for the baby, I climbed into the ambulance. I wanted to be sure I was not left behind. After what seemed an eternity, the grim procession moved slowly out the door. One of the white-coated attendants bent over the stretcher, continuing to coax air into the frail lungs. As we sped toward the hospital, I kept looking to Gene for reassurance that Bobby John was still alive.

The ambulance driver had called in "code blue," meaning death is imminent. When we reached the emergency entrance of the hospital, the walkway was lined with a team of doctors and nurses. All I could do was thank God for His provision. They took Bobby John and were gone in a flash down a corridor, leaving Gene and me numb with shock and disbelief.

A lady from the admissions office appeared, requesting the routine information. The three of us sat down, the lady from admissions between us. Suddenly, I stopped her in the middle of a question and asked if she would wait just a moment so Gene and I could pray for our son. We joined hands and turned Bobby John over to God. Choking over the words, we told Him we would accept His will for our lives. He would be no less our God if Bobby John died. The lady sitting between us began to cry too. No sooner had we said "Amen" than we heard a loud and beautiful sound from the direction of the examining room where they had taken Bobby John. Through his own tears, Gene said, "Cry, son, cry!"

By the time Bobby John had been transferred to the Intensive Care Unit of All Children's Hospital, it was two o'clock in the morning. Gene stayed with him that night while I went home to the other two boys whom I had left in Jenny's care.

Thad, our middle son, was still sleeping when I got home. But Travis was wide awake, frightened, and certain that Bobby John was dead. Jenny had tried to calm him, but it was several hours before he could settle down enough to sleep.

During the trying week that followed, God provided human channels for His love. Gene's mother flew down from Jacksonville to take care of the other children. Christian friends stood by with words of encouragement, enabling us to endure the week of waiting while the doctors determined if Bobby John had suffered brain damage. None of us were sure just how long he had been without oxygen.

Several times during that week I was again overwhelmed by fear. When I needed to share my feelings, God always provided someone. My sister, Neva, called long distance often, just at the times I needed her most. God's comforting hand was upon us through so many people.

It was discovered that Bobby John had a brain dysfunction that caused his brain to shut down when he ran a high fever. The soft palate in his throat had also collapsed, making artificial respiration ineffective. When Gene cut Bobby John's throat with the rusty razor blade, it had shocked the nerve endings, causing his brain to function again. We were told the shutdown could occur again any time he ran a fever. The doctor prescribed medication to prevent convulsions, or at least to reduce the severity. He was also given a medicine to be used only if his fever rose above 103 degrees. This medication could cause leukemia, and I shuddered the few times we had to use it.

You would think that after we brought Bobby John home from the hospital, we would have been filled with untold joy and relief. Just the opposite was true! I felt much safer when he was in the hospital surrounded by competent nurses and doctors. Nights became almost unbearable for Gene and me. Every sound the baby made sent us running into his room. We were all very much aware of the fact that had we not found him last time exactly when we did, he would have died quietly in his sleep. Perhaps we wouldn't hear him the next time. Perhaps he would convulse while we slept. The fear was disabling—robbing me of rest and strength.

I shared my situation with our minister's wife. She told me that I needed to pray for a scripture to claim—one I could cling to during these moments of terror. She and I prayed together that God would reveal His special word to me.

One night Gene went to sleep before I did. I lay in bed frozen with fear! Every time Bobby John turned in his crib, I died a little, imagining him fighting for breath. Finally, I could stand it no longer and went into the living room to read my Bible. I simply picked it up and opened it at random. I began to read in the seventh chapter of Luke. The words **funeral procession** jumped from the page, taunting me with their hopelessness. I told God I didn't want to read about a funeral. He urged me to continue. I read how Jesus raised from the dead the son of a widow. The story told of Jesus' great compassion for the mother and how He "gave (the son) back to his mother." There was my scripture!

I closed my Bible and rested my head against the chair, eyes brimming with tears of gratitude. I went to bed and slept as I had not slept in weeks.

It has been my experience that ninety percent of the things I worry about never happen. Yet, sometimes I find myself worrying anyway "just in case." However, as a Christian, I have discovered that God is the only insurance I need against the storms of life. So, I am learning to confess my fears to my Father, knowing He will handle them as only He can.

I love the scripture that reads "Satan is like a roaring lion." Hunters tell us that a roaring lion is a sick and toothless animal who has only his roar left to frighten his prey. The old lion boldly approaches a herd and fiercely roars his head off, forcing the prey to dart into the waiting clutches of the young lions. Then the old lion comes in to eat his fill. Little did the helpless victims know that their cowardice was responsible for their downfall! Had they run toward the object of their fear, they would have been saved.

> Fear not, for I am with you. Do not be dismayed. I am your God. I will strengthen you; I will help you; I will uphold you with my victorious right hand (Isa. 41:10, TLB).

That scripture passage makes me want to shout for joy! He **is** with us. He **does** strengthen, help, uphold, and give victory—**if** we ask Him. As long as we hide our need and refuse to admit our weakness, He will let us struggle alone. But the instant we turn to Him, He lifts the burden from our shoulders.

Fear marches in when we assume a responsibility that is not ours. At that moment, we must stop and consciously discern where our responsibility in the matter ends and God's begins. By following this formula, we can conquer this night stalker of the human spirit.

## LIFELINES

**When fear strikes, the following passages from God's Word offer twenty-four-hour protection:**

☆

Yes, though a mighty army marches against me, my heart shall know no fear! I am confident that God will save me (Ps. 27:3, TLB).

☆

He is for me! How can I be afraid? What can mere man do to me (Ps. 118:6, TLB)?

☆

Fear of man is a dangerous trap, but to trust in God means safety (Prov. 29:25, TLB).

☆

See, God has come to save me! I will trust and not be afraid, for the Lord is my strength and song; he is my salvation (Isa. 12:2, TLB).

☆

But now the Lord who created you, O Israel, says, Don't be afraid, for I have ransomed you; I have called you by name; you are mine. When you go through deep waters and great trouble, I will be with you. When you go through rivers of difficulty, you will not drown! When you walk through the fire of oppression, you will not be burned up—the flames will not consume you (Isa. 43:1-2, TLB).

☆

What can we ever say to such wonderful things as these? If God is on our side, who can ever be against us (Rom. 8:31, TLB)?

# Chapter 2

# Today, Lord, Today!
## (Impatience)

I have discovered that I'm only impatient when I have to wait! I'm the kind of person who never does tomorrow what I can do today. I never write letters when I can use the telephone. I bake pound cakes that are gooey in the middle because I can't wait for anything to bake one hour! So God provided a situation for me through which my patience could grow.

It all started when I began writing the book, **Till the Apple Turns Red.** After months of working almost nonstop on the manuscript, it was finally ready to mail to a publisher. From the beginning of the project, I knew in my heart that Warner Press would publish my book. Why I felt that way I really don't know.

After mailing the manuscript, I waited for six weeks without hearing a word. No one had told me that in publishing circles six to eight weeks of reviewing and evaluating unsolicited material is considered routine. I couldn't stand the suspense any longer, so I asked Gene if I could call Warner Press to inquire about my manuscript. Understanding how I felt and anxious himself, he gave his approval. I planned what I would say, uttered a quick three-word prayer, and dialed the number. The conversation went like this:

"Warner Press."

"May I speak to Dr. Phillips?"

"Just a moment, please."

"Hello," came a cool, female voice. "This is Dr. Phillips' office."

"May I speak to Dr. Phillips?"

"One moment, please." She transferred the call to the inner sanctum.

"Dr. Phillips speaking." His voice was abrupt and very businesslike. I could just picture him sitting there in his pin-striped, vested suit, obviously annoyed by the interruption.

"Dr. Phillips, this is Cyvette Guerra."

"Who?"

I just wanted to hang up and pretend the call had never taken place! With that question, my hopes were shattered. My book was surely not going to be published by Warner Press. But I forged ahead.

"Cyvette Guerra. I wrote **Till the Apple Turns Red.** I was just wondering if you ever received my manuscript?"

After a frightening pause, he replied, "Yes, I did. Sorry we are so long in contacting you, but we have a book contest going on now, and I have about one hundred manuscripts sitting on my desk."

Did I hear him right? I asked myself. A hundred manuscripts! A contest! However, Dr. Phillips was kind enough to tell me he had received a favorable report from the first reader. He then assured me I would hear from him soon. My idea of **soon** was **tomorrow.** His idea was more like **six weeks**! I was reluctantly learning patience.

Four weeks after the phone call, I could easily have been described as paranoid. I just knew the mailman was hiding that letter from me. Every night I committed the mailman and his precious delivery to God, only to snatch it all back in the morning. My entire life revolved around the ten o'clock mail.

Finally, after six agonizing weeks, the letter came. I couldn't believe I was actually holding it in my hand. I was afraid to open it. The letter informed me that Warner Press was considering the book for mass paperback; therefore, a copy had to be sent to New York for a reading there. The letter also stated that this process would take "awhile." Again my idea of **awhile** and theirs was considerably different! Six weeks later I was literally about to explode! I had to know! So I placed another long distance call.

The conversation that followed was one of the most embarrassing of my life. I said all the wrong things, called Dr. Phillips "Dr. Warner," and made a total idiot of myself. However, I did learn that Pyramid Press in New York liked the book and planned to publish it in mass paperback. It seemed that my lifelong dream was to become a reality after all.

Many problems were yet to come. The paper shortage hit, and the economic downturn which affected the entire publishing industry did not spare Warner Press. Not only that, but periodically I continued to call Dr. Phillips, pushing him for decisions he could not possibly make. Finally, I must have pushed Dr. Phillips to the brink! I received a letter that informed me Warner was not going to be able to publish the book after all. The letter was very apologetic and never implied that I had driven them to despair, but I knew. The last part of the letter made it final—the manuscript was being returned to me.

The death of a vision is almost as painful as a death in the family. That book was born of long hours and hard labor. But it was not the fault of Warner Press or Dr. Phillips. It was my fault, and there was no other place to put the blame. I was embarrassed and ashamed as God began to show me the side of myself that tended to run stubbornly ahead of His will.

I prayed for new direction, but it would not come. Finally, I felt impressed to write Dr. Phillips and admit to him that I knew why he had changed his mind about publishing the book. I also sent the manuscript along with the letter, giving them unlimited time to publish the book if they were still interested.

When I dropped that manuscript in the mail, I sent my overconcern right along with it. My job was over. I had written the book and the final outcome was not my responsibility. No longer did I have uncontrollable urges to make long distance calls to Warner Press. The months rolled by and I heard nothing. I didn't even know if the manuscript had arrived, but somehow it just didn't matter.

During this time my motives were tested and purified. It was necessary for God to break my pride so that His perfect will could be done. I still felt in my heart that God would see that the book was published, but it would be **in His own time.** I sincerely believed that He had led me to write. I also believed that this book would minister to those who read it, since I had written honestly out of my own searching.

Six months after I mailed the manuscript, Dr. Phillips called me one morning to tell me that Warner Press was going to publish the book. After all my rash phone calls to him, it was nice to receive such a call!

Lessons of growth are always painful and never come easily. Yet the rewards gained far surpass the pain involved. A minister friend, Dr. Maurice Berquist, once said, "Unless you're willing to face deep problems, you'll never realize deep possibilities." Centuries before, another wise man had said:

> Finishing is better than starting! Patience is better than pride! Don't be quick-tempered—that is being a fool (Eccl. 7:8, TLB).

Our society lends itself to impatience. Everything, it seems, must be done in a hurry! Even things that are designed to relax us are "improved" until a gadget is created that does it faster! Faster! Faster! Faster! It is easy to see how this philosophy carries over into our spiritual lives as well.

Yet our God is a God of patience. He is never in a hurry. He will not dash along beside us, trying to get our attention. If we are to hear His voice and feel His presence, we must slow down to His pace.

> Come to me and I will give you rest—all of you who work so hard beneath a heavy yoke. Wear my yoke—for it fits perfectly—and let me teach you; for I am gentle and humble, and you shall find rest for your souls; for I give you only light burdens (Matt. 11:28-30, TLB).

The pressure comes when we are "working," and God is asking us to wait! For God gives only "light burdens."

In **The Christian's Secret of a Happy Life**, Hannah Whitall Smith tells the story of a man who had a great burden to carry. As he was forced to move and had no wagon or mule to carry his belongings, he strapped them on his back and began his long journey. After traveling for many days, a man happened by driving a team of horses pulling an empty wagon. The driver felt sorry for the weary traveler and stopped to offer him a ride. Gratefully, the man accepted and pulled himself onto the wagon. After awhile, the driver of the wagon realized his rider had not removed the great load from his back. He continued to sit there, his shoulders slumped under the burden. Finally, the man said, "Sir, why don't you loosen your pack and simply lay it in the wagon?" With that the stranger replied, "Oh, I couldn't do that. You've been so kind already. I couldn't possibly take advantage of your goodness."

Isn't it ironic that we relinquish our souls to God but don't trust Him with our daily lives? We are so caught up in the do-it-yourself philosophy so prevalent in our society that we can't unstrap the burdens from our backs, even though we are already riding in the wagon!

The Christian experience is to be one of resting (as in "waiting on the Lord")—not tugging, pulling, sweating, and worrying. Pagan peoples have to carry their idols. Our God can carry us!

It was a revelation to learn that God cares about every detail of our complex lives. As this truth began to dawn for me, I was able to surrender more and more problem areas to Him.

I remember one instance that taught me just how much God does care about the "little things." Gene and I had bought carpet for our living room, dining room, and hallway. It was quite an investment for us. The carpet had been down only a matter of weeks when we noticed that all the traffic areas showed signs of extreme wear. On further examination we could see that each separate strand had frayed. We called the store where we had purchased it. The owner came out to examine the carpet and agreed that it did look bad, but said he was not in a position to correct the situation. He explained that he owned a small store and could not absorb the loss. He did contact the manufacturer of the carpet but they, too, refused to replace it.

My natural inclination was to grab the picket signs and go to work! I could make certain that neither the manufacturer nor the dealer got any business again. That was the old Cyvette. But I checked the impulse and asked God what He would have me do. His Word was waiting for me.

Always be thankful no matter what happens, for this is God's will for you who belong to Christ Jesus (1 Thess. 5:18, TLB).

I thought it was time to try that scripture on for size. So Gene and I dismissed the matter from our minds, leaving it with the Lord. We agreed to keep the frayed carpet if God wanted us to. We would do nothing on our own to force the company to replace it.

Weeks passed and nothing happened. I had already resigned myself to the fact that the carpet, worn spots and all, was ours. Then one day the phone rang. It was the dealer informing us our carpet was going to be replaced. The manufacturer had been bought out by another firm who wanted to make our purchase good. I couldn't believe my ears! Not only was the carpet replaced, but with a brand several dollars per yard more expensive than the original.

Dear brothers, is your life full of difficulties and temptations? Then be happy, for when the way is rough, your patience has a chance to grow . . . and don't try to squirm out of your problems. For when your patience is finally in full bloom, then you will be ready for anything, strong in character, full and complete (Jas. 1:2-4. TLB).

# LIFELINES

**If you need patience and you need it now, slow down and listen to the One who never hurries.**

☆

We can rejoice, too, when we run into problems and trials for we know that they are good for us—they help us learn to be patient. And patience develops strength of character in us and helps us trust God more each time we use it until finally our hope and faith are strong and steady (Rom. 5:3-4, TLB).

☆

Run from all these evil things and work instead at what is right and good, learning to trust him and love others, and to be patient and gentle (1 Tim. 6:11, TLB).

☆

Then, knowing what lies ahead for you, you won't become bored with being a Christian, nor become spiritually dull and indifferent, but you will be anxious to follow the example of those who receive all that God has promised them because of their strong faith and patience (Heb. 6:12, TLB).

☆

Do not let this happy trust in the Lord die away, no matter what happens. Remember your reward! You need to keep on patiently doing God's will if you want him to do for you all that he has promised (Heb. 10:35-36, TLB).

# Chapter 3
# "My" Will Be Done
## (Disobedience)

When Gene felt that God was calling him as a ministerial student to Asbury College in Wilmore, Kentucky, I was scared to death! I had never lived outside the state of Florida in my entire life. What would I do without sand between my toes or the surf only a stone's throw away? What would I do when the urge to visit Mom and Dad became bigger than our budget? Nor would I be able to see my older sister, Neva, whenever I wanted.

I knew I must obey my husband and God—I certainly wanted to, but I was apprehensive about the future. I realized I did not possess the strength nor the power to be obedient to that calling. The price seemed to high. That was before I studied about Abraham.

Abraham's life story was a challenging example of pulling up roots and taking off into unfamiliar territory with nothing more than the clear call of God. Without even knowing his final destination, Abraham moved lock, stock, and barrel; herds, tents, and family in the direction of God's leading.

For Abraham's faith and trust grew ever stronger, and he praised God for this blessing even before it happened. He was completely sure that God was well able to do anything he promised (Rom. 4:20-21, TLB).

And in thy seed shall all the nations of the earth be blessed; because thou hast obeyed my voice (Gen. 22:18).

God did not say He would bless Abraham because he was such a nice guy or because he was better than anyone else. **God blessed Abraham because he was obedient!** At least I knew where my new home would be; and when I finally prayed, "Lord, help me to be obedient to your call; I want to follow you," the joy came flooding back.

When God speaks, the temptation is to turn a deaf ear, fearing that what He asks is too demanding or impractical. We forget that He will supply the power as well as the plan.

I remember the first time Gene and I began to tithe. God had made it clear in various ways that this was what He wanted us to do. When we dropped that fifty-dollar check into the offering plate for the first time, I felt faint! Fifty dollars! We had never given fifty dollars to anything before. Surely God could not expect so much. Yet that amount was only a portion of what we should have been giving. Financially, we had to work gradually toward the ten percent. Within six months God had made it possible not only for us to tithe but also to give beyond the tithe. Still we wondered how we would survive without that money. Then we discovered a passage in Proverbs:

My son, forget not my law; but let thine heart keep my commandments: for length of days, and long life, and peace, shall they add to thee. Let not mercy and truth forsake thee: bind them about thy neck; write them upon the table of thine heart: So shalt thou find favour and good understanding in the sight of God and man. Trust in the Lord with all thine heart and lean not unto thine own understanding (Prov. 3:1-5).

Wow! Did you count the promises in those verses? Long life, peace, favor in the sight of God . . . He provides the power to be obedient and then blesses us for obeying.

I read on, now completely captivated by the inviting promises:

> Then shalt thou walk in thy way safely, and thy foot shall not stumble. When thou liest down, thou shalt not be afraid: Yea, thou shalt lie down, and thy sleep shall be sweet. Be not afraid of sudden fear, neither of the desolation of the wicked, when it cometh. For the Lord shall be thy confidence and shall keep thy foot from being taken (Prov. 3:23-26).

Lack of fear; sweet, peaceful sleep; confidence; boldness in the face of evil—ours for the asking if we trust and obey. Warning! These promises are reserved for obedient believers only.

Obedience is the heartbeat of Christianity. It is a fallacy of our day to think that all a person has to do to become a Christian is to believe. No wonder so many people claim to be Christians—it is easy to believe. Yet if you ask, "What does it mean to be a Christian?" many are at a total loss to define the term. Certainly the word **obedience** would not be a part of that definition. How can you win people to Christ when they think they are already saved?

During Holy Week services at our church, the speaker gave us a mini-lesson in Greek. One of the problems in translating Greek to English, he explained, is that we leave behind much of the rich meaning inherent in each word. For example, in the Greek language, the connotation of the word **believe** is **obey**. Therefore, believing always involves obedience.

Try this. In the following scripture, substitute the word **obey** for the word **believe.**

> For God so loved the world that he gave his only Son, that whoever believes (obeys) in him should not perish but have eternal life (John 3:16, RSV).

Our salvation and eternal destiny are determined by our understanding of that basic verse. So, too, is our Christian growth.

As Christians grow toward maturity, obedience continues to be a vital building block. When, for example, we are tested beyond our endurance, the mature Christian will ask for the power to be obedient. When we ask Him for that power, we are saying, "God, I don't understand but I trust you. I know you're in control. Give me the power to be what you want me to be." And God's answer to that prayer is a cup of overflowing joy.

> "I have loved you even as the Father has loved me. Live within my love. When you **obey** me you are living in my love, just as I **obey** my Father and live in his love. I have told you this so that you will be filled with my joy. Yes, your cup of joy will overflow" (John 15:9-11, TLB).

Did you find the **one** condition for receiving joy that knows no bounds? The clue is contained in this passage. To experience that joy we must practice obedience to our heavenly Father, remembering that **He** provides the power.

Indifference is a deadly form of disobedience. The indifferent person is one who has lost his first love. He is no longer excited about Jesus Christ and all He stands for. This person has slipped into a halfhearted Christian experience that excites no one, including himself. God calls this professing Christian "lukewarm."

> "I know you well—you are neither hot nor cold; I wish you were one or the other! But since you are merely lukewarm, I will spit you out of my mouth" (Rev. 3:15-16, TLB).

God pronounces severe judgment on this type of disobedience. When a person professes to be a Christian, he takes on the name and reputation of Christ; just as in marriage, one's name belongs to or becomes coupled with that of his spouse. From that moment on, the actions of one reflects on the other. The same is true when we profess to be Christians. We are the witnessing body of Jesus Christ on this earth.

> And whatever you do or say, let it be as a representative of the Lord Jesus (Col. 3:17, TLB).

It's sad but true that often those who lead people **away** from the cross are not nonbelievers but lukewarm Christians. They tell people they are Christians and then act as if they are not. The nonbeliever comes to the understandable but wrong conclusion that Christ has no answers for life either! More **Christians** have hurt the cause of Christianity than non-Christians ever have or ever will!

Another trap that snares some Christians is the belief that we can do as we please and expect God to clean up our mess. That idea has no basis in Christ's teachings. God provided us with His holy Word to keep us from making life-altering errors. God can forgive, but He cannot undo! Once we have decided to be disobedient, we are then willfully stepping out from under His umbrella of protection. Like a murderer who has accepted Jesus Christ as his Savior, God can save the soul but He cannot erase the prison term. He can forgive the sin, but He is often powerless to eliminate the consequence of that sin. That is precisely why God exhorts us over and over again to obey His Word.

> Not every one that saith unto me, Lord, Lord, shall enter into the kingdom of heaven; but he that **doeth** the will of my Father which is in heaven (Matt. 7:21).

This is not to say that we will never sin again. It does mean that we will not deliberately continue to commit the **same** sins. That belongs to the life left behind! But at any given moment, you and I can be disobedient in some area, only to find that we must then suffer the natural consequences of that attitude or action.

Not long after moving to Kentucky, I had an automobile accident while taking some clothes to a lady who was to do some ironing for me. As I drove along the unfamiliar streets, searching for the house number, I ran a stop sign. Suddenly, I heard the squeal of brakes. When I looked up, I saw a speeding car just seconds before impact. I had just enough time to call upon Jesus. He put His hand of protection on me. The car that hit me was traveling 45 or 50 mph, yet I suffered no serious injury.

For a long time I did not understand why God allowed that accident to happen. I had come to understand that God is in control of **all** things that affect those who love Him; therefore, I could not understand why He had not intervened. Our car had received $1,500 damage and was in the body shop for some time, leaving me without transportation to and from work. Gene had the extra burden of coming for me in the afternoon. Being a pastor, husband, father, and full-time student left little time for another task. I was grateful God had saved my life, but I just couldn't understand why He had permitted this added pressure when we already had more than our share!

As I was considering this one day, it suddenly occurred to me that God had not allowed the accident at all. By running the stop sign, I was leaving myself wide open for the consequences. If I had obeyed the sign, I might possibly have avoided the accident altogether. It was Christ who stepped in and spared my life when I so foolishly left His realm of protection.

Smoking is a good example of deliberate disobedience to God's will for our lives. There is not a smoker living who does not know smoking is extremely hazardous to his health. So, when a smoker develops cancer, can we say God allowed it? Of course not. The cancer in this case is a consequence of disobedience. It is tragic that we can, by violating the basic laws of nature, shorten our lives before our work is finished.

As a non-Christian, I tried to quit smoking hundreds of times. I couldn't do it. I was so hooked on cigarettes I felt I would die without them. I reasoned that smoking was my one pleasure in life as I struggled to raise three small children.

Not long after accepting Christ, I could almost hear Him telling me I was ruining the body He had given me. Already I had been ill with pneumonia and pleurisy twice. Under conviction, I prayed, asking God to give me the power to stop smoking. Suddenly, I discovered I could stop! Once I decided to be **obedient,** God did the rest.

Several weeks later, I shared this testimony at church—the first time I was able to proclaim God's Word in action in my own life. It stands out in my mind as a great moment. I knew then that God would supply all the power I needed to live my life as He desired. All I had to do was decide if I **wanted** to be obedient.

No, dear brothers, I am still not all I should be but I am bringing all my energies to bear on this one thing: Forgetting the past and looking forward to what lies ahead, I strain to reach the end of the race and receive the prize for which God is calling (Phil. 3:13-14, TLB).

# LIFELINES

**If you're the stubborn kind, take notice of these warnings and promises from God's Word.**

☆

Now if you will obey me and keep your part of my contract with you, you shall be my own little flock from among all the nations of the earth (Ex. 19:5, TLB).

☆

Obey me and I will be your God and you shall be my people; only do as I say and all shall be well (Jer. 7:23, TLB)!

☆

The one who obeys me is the one who loves me; and because he loves me, my Father will love him; and I will too, and I will reveal myself to him (John 14:21, TLB).

☆

When you obey me you are living in my love, just as I obey my Father and live in his love (John 15:10, TLB).

☆

And how can we be sure that we belong to him? By looking within ourselves: are we really trying to do what he wants us to? Someone may say, "I am a Christian; I am on my way to heaven; I belong to Christ." But if he doesn't do what Christ tells him to, he is a liar. But those who do what Christ tells them to will learn to love God more and more (1 John 2:3-5, TLB).

# Chapter 4

# Why Me, Lord?
## (Murmuring)

I really struggled with the proper subtitle for this chapter. I was a little afraid of the word **murmur** because of its heavy theological tone. So, I toyed with other words like **complaining** or **griping,** but they lacked the depth of meaning necessary to convey the idea. Murmuring is an inward-outward cry that is stifled to an undertone by the time it reaches our vocal cords. Murmuring betrays inner attitudes. It is a mirror of hidden feelings that reflects the real person inside. Complaining or griping might be a sudden reaction to an unexpected irritation that soon passes. When that happens, we often feel guilty for having given in to the momentary irritation. When we murmur, however, we feel no remorse or guilt but find ourselves justifying the response.

The childen of Israel were guilty of murmuring. The minute the going got a little rough, they began to murmur against God for having led them out of Egypt. Once they learned the price of their freedom, they accused Moses of taking them into the wilderness to die. They preferred to eat in shackles and know the meal was coming than to wait for God's miracle manna to drop from heaven each day.

I used to read the story of the Exodus and shake my head sympathetically, "Poor God, how did you ever put up with such rebellious, ungrateful people?" I quit throwing stones when I discovered that I, too, am often guilty of the same kind of ingratitude.

After moving to Kentucky, I began a little business called The New for You—a quality used clothing store. People would bring me their good, used clothing to be sold on consignment. I split the amount received for each garment with the consignee. The shop did extremely well in a very short time. After the first month, we were making what I had hoped to make in two years! I just simply could not believe my good fortune.

Do you think I clicked my heels with happiness? I should have, but I didn't. I didn't want to work so much. I didn't like the responsibility of running the shop. I didn't want to work **at all.** I was like the people of Israel at the crossing of the Red Sea. I was amazed and astounded at the miracle God performed for me; but on the other side, my amazement soon dissolved into tears of discontent and ingratitude.

> And don't murmur against God and his dealings with you, as some of them did, for that is why God sent his Angel to destroy them (1 Cor. 10:10, TLB).

In equally record time the shop began to fail. Proceeds from the business dropped one-half from the previous month. Then the next month, they dropped again. Soon the dollars were just trickling in. Bills began to mount. It looked as if the shop would fold.

As the situation with the shop deteriorated, I found myself throwing scriptures at God: Didn't you say you would fulfill the desires of my heart? Didn't you say you would meet all my needs? Didn't you say, "Seek ye first the kingdom of God and all these things will be added unto you? " Why then, God, aren't you doing what you said you would?

Though I didn't blatantly confront God with my dissatisfaction as to how He was handling things, these thoughts plagued my subconscious mind. On one hand, the thoughts were disturbing; on the other, I figured I had a pretty good point! After all, wasn't Gene studying for the ministry under the most trying of conditions? Wasn't I the wife who had followed him to a remote rural community and was now trying to help support the family?

I prayed for God to reveal what He was trying to teach me. (When you pray, be prepared for unexpected answers!) In rereading the story of the children of Israel, I discovered, to my horror, that I was **just** like them.

I sincerely asked God's forgiveness. Whether the shop survived or not was no longer important. In spite of God's goodness, I had been ungrateful. Like a spoiled child, I no longer appreciated His wonderful gifts of love. I **expected** them—and more!

The point is, God **had** provided for our needs. We had not missed one meal. We had never been without plenty of warm clothing. We had a roof over our heads. Yes, God had done what He promised to do.

I was told once that Satan is a great quoter of scripture. He has a subtle way of reciting in our ears the parts of the Scriptures that speak of what God said He would do and leaving out **our** part! We forget that before God can fulfill His promises, our hearts must be right before Him. How could God continue to bless the shop when I was being such an ungrateful, spoiled child?

Do all things without murmurings and disputings: That ye
may be blameless and harmless, the sons of God, without
rebuke, in the midst of a crooked and perverse nation,
among whom ye shine as lights in the world (Phil.
2:14-15).

During this financial crisis, Gene had an in-
teresting discussion with a fellow student at Asbury
College. The student, who is Gene's age, is married
and the father of two children. Like Gene, he had felt
the call into the ministry at the age of thirty-three.
The previous year he had had a job that amply supplied all his family's needs. Now, while he was in
school, his wife was supporting the family.

The problem began when she lost her job. With
the electric bill past due, the company was threaten-
ing to turn off their power. Not only that, there was
very little in the house to eat and no money for
groceries.

Gene's friend was discouraged and disillusioned.
He had taken some pretty big risks for God. Now
look at the mess he was in! He was beginning to
doubt that God could solve a problem this big.

We continued to pray for the student and his family. The next Sunday Gene shared their story with
our congregation. As pastor, he felt God leading him
to ask for a love offering. The response was overwhelming! Not only was enough money given to pay
the electric bill, but enough for a week's groceries as
well.

Gene did not tell his friend what God had laid on
his heart. Therefore, the student didn't know that an
offering was going to be taken in his behalf. He sat
around all weekend feeling depressed and wondering why God had failed him while the provision for
his needs was already being made!

After much soul searching, this young man discovered that he had put a condition on becoming a

minister of the gospel. He had told God if this idea didn't work out, he would go back to his previous life and forget all about serving Him. When he came to terms with himself and his attitudes, he realized that God was trying to teach him a valuable lesson in faith. (Only God can show you something shocking about yourself and make you feel better for knowing it!)

It is difficult to trust God when we cannot see beyond our immediate problems. Yet these are opportunities for growth. Each time I pass through such an experience, my faith grows. Next time I am able to trust a little more. I look forward to the day when my faith in God is so solid that I will not waver, no matter what situation I face. I will know beyond question that God is sufficient for any need, because He has proved Himself so many times in the past.

When faced with problems that tempt me to murmur, I have learned to ask: **What is God trying to teach me through this situation?** He does not allow problems to come into our lives to frustrate and irritate us. He is using these experiences to tell us something! For example, when you punish your children for misbehaving, what are you trying to accomplish? Are you spanking and scolding just to be mean? Certainly not! Do you send them to their rooms so they can miss their favorite TV show? Ridiculous! No, you want them to learn something. You hope they will be able to say, "I get it! I see what you're trying to teach me." The moment they can grasp the message, the punishment is no longer necessary.

As loving parents, it is sometimes necessary to teach our children the hard way. God is willing to do that for us also. He is motivated by love so that our happiness may be full and our joy complete!

Dear friends, don't be bewildered or surprised when you go through the fiery trials ahead, for this is no strange, unusual thing that is going to happen to you. Instead, be **really glad**—because these trials will make you partners with Christ in his suffering, and afterwards you will have the wonderful joy of sharing his glory in that coming day when it will be displayed (1 Pet. 4:12-13, TLB).

Every time God teaches me a painful lesson, I see His face a little more clearly and I am "really glad" for the trial. I find out something about myself that was robbing me of the joy of belonging to Him. Someone once put it this way: "God loved me enough to accept me the way I am, but He loved me too much to leave me that way!"

When the channels of communication break down between ourselves and God, perhaps the problem stems from murmuring. The children of Israel slammed the door shut in God's face when they murmured against Him. God didn't go anywhere. He continued to provide for them, but they lost the joy of fellowship with Him.

Martin Luther, in a fit of anger, once complained that if he were God and the world treated him as it had treated God, he would have kicked the wretched thing to pieces long ago. Instead, Christ chose to die for us, "while we were yet sinners."

It is startling to realize that we can disappoint God. Many people have not learned that He is moved, not only by our afflictions, but by our thoughtlessness and thanklessness.

When the Lord God saw the extent of human wickedness, and that the trend and direction of men's lives were only towards evil, he was sorry he had made them. It broke his heart (Gen. 6:5-6, TLB).

God's heart is breakable. He is not some unemotional, uncaring, get-even ruler just waiting to slap our hands when we step out of line. He has a personal stake in the success or failure of His children. Just as we long for our children to reach their fullest potential, so God desires that ultimate goal for us. Oh, that we could care for Him as deeply.

How, then, do we keep from murmuring? By developing a spirit of true gratitude. By realizing that each new day is a gift—that all we have, are, and ever hope to be is a direct result of His caring. If we can't run, then let's be thankful we can walk. If we can't walk, then let's praise Him that we can crawl. If we can't crawl, then let's rejoice in the fact that we are still breathing. A truly grateful heart will always find a way to praise!

# LIFELINES

**Counting blessings is the perfect antidote to complaining and murmuring.**

☆

Shout with joy before the Lord, O earth! Obey him gladly; come before him singing with joy . . . the Lord is God! He made us—we are his people, the sheep of his pasture. Go through his open gates with real thanksgiving; enter his courts with praise. Give thanks to him and bless his name. For the Lord is always good. He is always loving and kind, and his faithfulness goes on and on to each succeeding generation (Ps. 100, TLB).

☆

A man may ruin his chances by his own foolishness and then blame it on the Lord (Prov. 19:3, TLB)!

☆

For God is at work within you, helping you want to obey him, and then helping you do what he wants. In everything you do, stay away from complaining and arguing (Phil. 2:13-14, TLB).

☆

Do you want to be truly rich? You already are if you are happy and good. After all, we didn't bring any money with us when we came into the world, and we can't carry away a single penny when we die. So we should be well satisfied without money if we have enough food and clothing (1 Tim. 6:6-8, TLB).

☆

Stay away from the love of money; be satisfied with what you have. For God has said, "I will never, never fail you nor forsake you" (Heb. 13:5, TLB).

# Chapter 5

# **You've Got To Be Kidding!**
## (Doubt)

| | |
|---|---|
| THE OTHER DISCIPLES: | We have seen the Lord! |
| THOMAS: | Except I shall see in his hands the print of the nails, and put my finger into the print of the nails, and thrust my hand into his side, I will not believe! |
| THE OTHER DISCIPLES: | Thomas, you gotta be kiddin'! |
| THOMAS: | I will not believe until I see and feel the scars. |
| THE OTHER DISCIPLES: | It'll snow in June before you see those scars! You're just going to have to take our word for it. Jesus is alive! |
| THOMAS: | I will not believe! |

Eight days later:

| | |
|---|---|
| JESUS: | Thomas, Reach hither thy finger, and behold my hands; and reach hither thy hand, and thrust it into my side: and be not faithless, but believing. |
| THOMAS: | My Lord and my God! |
| THE OTHER DISCIPLES: | We told you! |
| JESUS: | Thomas, because thou hast seen me, thou hast believed: blessed are they that have not seen, and yet have believed. (Portions from John 20:25-29, KJV). |

**I will not believe!** Thomas was a realist. He had seen Jesus hanging on the cross. He knew where every wound had been inflicted on His body. He had seen Jesus take His last breath and utter those words of finality, "It is finished." Jesus was dead. It would take more than a few excited disciples to convince him otherwise.

Eight days later the Savior Himself appeared and dispelled all doubt. He approached Thomas, called him by name, and invited him to feel the scars. Thomas became a believer!

We are all kin to Thomas at one time or another. We doggedly hang on to our unbelief, saying, "Show me, show me." Yet Jesus says, "Blessed are they that have not seen, and yet have believed!"

Don't get me wrong—doubt has its place. Honest doubt causes us to question, and questioning causes us to seek answers.

The kind of doubt I list among the joy robbers is unhealthy doubt—doubt that keeps us in a chronic state of confusion. We can become slaves to those doubts—doubts about our personal relationship to Christ, doubts about being forgiven, doubts about the hope of heaven. The habitual doubter is locked into a fierce battle with Satan who enjoys hurling spears of hopelessness. Why give him the satisfaction?

What do we do with a nagging doubt that plagues our minds constantly? Is there a way out? Emphatically yes! The provision that God has given is available to every believer. No one is left out. That provision given to fight the battle against doubt is our self-determination—our "will."

Like Thomas, we **decide** to believe! The fact that Thomas said "I will not" also meant he possessed the capacity to say "I will." It was his choice. Like Thomas, we often say "**I can't**" when what we really mean is "**I won't**."

A writer for **Decision** magazine made this intriguing statement: THERE IS ALWAYS MORE TO KNOWING THAN HUMAN KNOWING WILL EVER KNOW. I thought that neatly summed up the subject of doubt. Obviously, we cannot know all there is to know. God did not design life that way. We will always be discovering answers, only to discover all the things that are yet left to learn. There is no end to it. If we deal with one doubt, another will crop up. That process is part of growing and discovering the unsearchable riches of Christ.

Several years ago when Gene felt God's call into the ministry, he said that if he understood what he was reading in the Scriptures, he should sell everything he owned and prepare himself to preach the gospel. I told him to go and read it again! I wasn't too crazy about the idea. We had purchased our first home only two years before, and we were just getting it fixed like we wanted. We had three small sons; and to top it off, Gene was then thirty-one years of age. It just didn't make sense.

The year spent in preparation for this change in our lives was filled with doubts. I doubted whether God could provide financially for us as Gene undertook his studies. I doubted that I had the courage to leave my friends, family, and church. I just plain doubted! Even though I doubted, I realized that I had a choice to make. I could continue to doubt to the point that I refused to go (I will not), or I could claim God's Word as my authority and decide to trust. I decided to trust. I had to come to the realization that, unlike man, God has no limitations. He could meet our needs. Now, three years later, as Gene enters his senior year of studies, I can attest to the fact that I made the right decision.

A great many of the doubts we face today are brought about by an "intellectual" society. In the name of being "informed," we are subjected to all sorts of deceptive literature that is the work of the devil! I have heard some Christians encouraging others to read such material, "How can you decide whether it's valid or not if you haven't read it? It really gives you something to think about." So, wanting to be up on current topics, objective, and open-minded, we read a controversial book. Our minds were then bombarded by an avalanche of doubts that never should have existed. We asked for it!

Put an end to the (idea of) being saved by finding favor with an endless chain of . . . wild ideas that stir up questions and arguments instead of helping people accept God's plan of faith (1 Tim. 1:3-4, TLB).

God speaks to us sharply at this point. He warns us to keep our minds fixed on His teachings and to avoid "wild ideas that stir up questions and arguments." It is easy to leave ourselves wide open to doubt and confusion when we are sidetracked by the world's standards.

Another relevant doubt we face as Christians in the world today is the idea that the Bible is full of error. "How could a document be translated and passed down generation after generation without error?" critics ask. That idea originated with Satan. He's the guy who said it first, and you know how rumors spread! As a young Christian, I fell for that one myself.

Quite innocently, a friend and I decided that a portion of the scripture had gotten into the Bible by accident. Mark 16:15-20 speaks of a difficult doctrine. In part, it reads, "In my name shall they cast out devils; they shall speak with new tongues; They shall take up serpents; and if they drink any deadly thing, it shall not hurt them." My friend told me that he understood many biblical scholars believe that this section was simply "tacked on" to Mark's Gospel by someone else at a later date. Well, that theory fit comfortably with my own ideas concerning miracles, so he and I agreed that it must have been an addition. Surely you could not drink a "deadly thing" and remain unharmed.

Early the next morning my two-year-old son sneaked out of bed. He made his way quietly to the kitchen and climbed to the kitchen counter. From there he found my hiding place for all the family medicines. He swallowed a full bottle of cough medicine that had just been prescribed for our ten-year-old and about a half bottle of aspirin. On our dash to the Emergency Room, I prayed that God would make that scripture about drinking "deadly things" a reality for Bobby John. Bobby John never even got drowsy! In fact, he gave the people in the Emergency Room a terrible time as they treated him.

As soon as we got home from the hospital, I rushed to the phone. "Uh, Randy, you know that scripture we decided doesn't belong in the Bible?" I learned then that God wrote and preserved all of the Scriptures. Just because we cannot explain them all does not mean they do not belong there. Often we must grow into an understanding of God's Word through a "living" experience. Doubting the authority of God's Word is spiritual suicide!

I am not implying that we should put God to a foolish test by purposely drinking "a deadly thing" or by handling serpents. Far from it! But I am saying that His thoughts are higher than our thoughts. Therefore, we should not take it upon ourselves to dissect the scripture and remove all the parts that bother us.

It is inevitable that, as we move into deeper channels of understanding with Christ, we will experience doubt. That is a natural part of the growth process.

One of my greatest doubts after becoming a Christian concerned my emotional makeup. If God made me like I am, I reasoned, why did He give me such runaway emotions? I began to question His judgment. One night as I lay in bed discussing the problem with Him, I felt Him telling me to surrender all of my emotions to Him. It was unbelievably easy! From that moment on, I knew that my emotional experiences were just as God wanted them to be. So when I experienced an emotion, good or bad, I accepted it as from the hand of my Father. No more fighting. No more questions. A marvelous peace was mine. God, in that instance, had used a "doubt" to expose an uncommitted area of my life.

But suppose God had been unable to get through to me with a solution to my doubt? What then? Would I have quit believing in Him because I was up against a problem I could not solve? Many Christians do just that. "Well, that's it, God. I can't make any sense out of all this. I quit!" Others simply bail out emotionally, pulling the plug on their faith.

At other times when we're flying high in the power of the Lord, it's hard to imagine ever doubting again. Elijah must have felt that way. Standing boldly before the 450 prophets of Baal on Mount Carmel, his voice rang out, firm and sure: "Choose ye this day whom you will serve." The power of God rested squarely on his shoulders and he felt it. He feared no man. (A woman proved to be another matter!)

After the test of the sacrifices when God had displayed his mighty power over the pitiful prophets of Baal, Ahab returned home to Jezebel with the news. When she discovered that her prophets had been murdered, she vowed to have Elijah killed. Even in those days, it didn't take long for the word to reach Elijah that Jezebel was in hot pursuit. What did he do? Did he face her resolutely as he had the false prophets on Mount Carmel? Hardly! He ran like a scared rabbit and hid himself in a cave. Elijah had become a captive—not to Jezebel, but to doubt. Suddenly he doubted God's ability to protect him.

A doubtful mind will be as unsettled as a wave of the sea that is driven and tossed by the wind (Jas. 1:6, TLB).

Elijah's lapse of faith is a common failing. Few of us will ever be so strong in the Lord that doubt cannot challenge our security, often after moments of great victory. We might as well be prepared to deal with it when it comes.

# LIFELINES

**When doubt knocks at the door of your faith and asks to come in, draw comfort and confidence from these words:**

☆

Commit everything you do to the Lord. Trust him to help you do it and he will (Ps. 37:5, TLB).

☆

If you want favor with both God and man, and a reputation for good judgment and common sense, then trust the Lord completely; don't ever trust yourself (Prov. 3:4-5, TLB).

☆

You will find me when you seek me, if you look for me in earnest (Jer. 29:13, TLB).

☆

Beware then of your own hearts dear brothers, lest you find that they, too, are evil and unbelieving and are leading you away from the living God (Heb. 3:12, TLB).

☆

You can never please God without faith, without depending on him. Anyone who wants to come to God must believe that there is a God and that he rewards those who sincerely look for him (Heb. 11:6, TLB).

# Chapter 6

# Me, Myself, and I
## (Selfishness)

Soon after moving to Paint Lick, which was smack dab in the middle of nowhere as far as I was concerned, I was horrified to discover that I was married to a "stranger." My once loving and attentive husband was now overworked, exhausted, and preoccupied with his new duties as full-time student and part-time pastor. No longer was I front and center in his life. I had left family and lifelong friends to come to this rural community and needed his companionship and support more than ever. But he simply did not have time to give me his undivided attention.

Before accepting Christ, I was constantly preoccupied with self. In fact my three favorite subjects were me, myself, and I. Gene, who loved me unselfishly, contributed to this state until his schedule no longer permitted the pampering.

So I spent a lot of time feeling sorry for myself in those first months. Didn't Gene love me anymore? Didn't he realize the sacrifice I was making? Did the boys really appreciate all I did for them? Poor little me.

I had always been concerned with what other people thought of me. After a conversation with friends, I would often grill myself unmercifully, Did I say the right thing? Had they understood what I meant? Was I accepted by the group? Just another version of the old self syndrome.

When Christ became my polestar, He freed me from much of that painful introspection. It was no longer necessary to be a slave to the expectations of others. He loved me just as I was.

Once I became aware of the fact that I was secure in the Lord's love, I was able to let "me" go. I no longer had to police myself to be sure everything was going all right. I left that up to God.

> O Lord, you have examined my heart and know everything about me. You know when I sit or stand. When far away you know my every thought. You chart the path ahead of me, and tell me where to stop and rest. Every moment, you know where I am. You know what I am going to say before I even say it. You both precede and follow me, and place your hand of blessing on my head . . . You made all the delicate, inner parts of my body, and knit them together in my mother's womb. Thank you for making me so wonderfully complex! You saw me before I was born and scheduled each day of my life before I began to breathe . . . How precious it is, Lord, to realize that you are thinking about me constantly! I can't even count how many times a day your thoughts turn towards me. And when I waken in the morning, you are still thinking of me. (Ps. 139: 1-5; 13-14; 16-18, TLB).

However, the lessons were not over after my conversion. As a matter of fact, they were just beginning. It was not easy for me to play second fiddle to Gene's new duties. It was even more difficult to put his needs before my own. But it was time I learned. Step by step, God led me to look beyond myself—to see with His eyes. It is still amazing to me that I received my new "sight" through Charlotte, one of God's smallest and most insignificant vessels.

Now Paint Lick is abundantly blessed with "critters." The surrounding fields and creeks teem with all kinds of wildlife—the fascinating red fox; small, furry things; birds of every description with an infinite variety of songs. In a household with three boys, the word was spread in the animal kingdom that the welcome mat is always out at the Guerras'. (Our most recent houseguest is a pigeon with a broken wing.)

As a city girl, it took some doing to become accustomed to living **this** close to nature. However, I was adjusting quite well—until Charlotte. If God were going to use an animal or insect as an object lesson, why did it have to be a **spider**?! I detest the things! Uninvited, she took up residence just outside our hallway window, wove herself an enormous web, and plopped down right in the middle as if she expected to be with us for a long time. I hated her long, hairy legs and obese body. Needless to say, the boys were delighted. Right away they gave her a name, adopted her, and trooped down the stairs each morning to see what juicy morsel their new pet had snared for breakfast. Often, she dined on grasshopper.

Despite my loathing for spiders, I began to watch Charlotte as she went about her daily chores. She really was rather pretty—for an insect. Her black and yellow markings were beautifully symmetrical. And I must admit she certainly knew how to keep house! Her web was an intricate pattern of silk that glistened with diamonds of dew in the morning sun. When she spun an egg sack, I was hooked. I could identify! One day it occurred to me that God had created Charlotte just as he wanted her to be; He had instilled in her the instincts to survive and to reproduce, and to make everything she touched more beautiful.

There are some people just like Charlotte. You may have to look hard to find the beauty, but it's there.

The first time I picked up the Bible as a new Christian, I was shocked to find such statements as "Love your enemies. Pray for those who persecute you!" Actually, it's much easier to hate the guy who hates you and to return evil for evil. And what about those like Charlotte—the unlovely ones we tend to ignore or, worse still, to shun?

As I began to read the Scriptures, especially the Gospels, I found a new pattern to live by. I found myself rerouting my life around the questions, "What would Jesus do? How did Jesus react when things went wrong? What was his attitude toward people who made demands on Him?" The most mind-boggling idea of all was His acceptance of death at the brutal hands of His persecuters.

I could picture Jesus hanging on the cross. I could see the people spitting on Him, scourging Him, mocking Him. I could see them standing at the foot of the cross, looking up into His suffering eyes, laughing at His pain, saying, "Save yourself if you are the Son of God." I cannot comprehend how Jesus continued to hang there when He had the power to do otherwise. I do not pretend to understand, but I do know that Jesus had to be more concerned for His persecutors than He was for Himself.

If Jesus could love His murderers with that kind of selfless love, then surely I could learn to love the gossipmongers, the critics, and even the unlovable people who entered my life.

Dear friends, let us practice loving each other, for love comes from God and those who are loving and kind show that they are the children of God, and that they are getting to know him better. But if a person isn't loving and kind, it shows that he doesn't know God—for God is love (1 John 4:7-8, TLB).

A distorted sense of self often blocks God's will in other life situations as well. I remember an experience in my childhood church in Jacksonville Beach, Florida. While visiting my parents, I attended Ocean Park Baptist Church with my sister. There were some familiar faces, some smiles of recognition. I discovered that all those years several members of that church had continued to pray for me.

Before the evening service, the minister asked if I would share my testimony and how I came to write my book, **Till the Apple Turns Red.** Much to my own amazement, I refused. I told the minister that I simply could not do that. I feared that my hands would shake, my voice would quiver, my knees would knock, and my mind would go blank. Yet I had become accustomed to stepping out on limbs with Christ. He had never disappointed me before. Why didn't I trust him now?

As I prayed about my hesitance, the answer became all too clear. I simply was not willing to risk making a spectacle of myself in front of my family and friends. I was not **willing** for my hands to shake, my knees to knock, or my mind to go blank. The other times I had followed Christ had not so openly threatened my image. Now with all the faith I could muster I said, "Yes, Lord, with your help I'll give it a try, even if I fail."

I spoke with the minister again and told him I had

changed my mind. I would be glad to share my testimony. My very first words were the confessions of an egotist—one who had been unwilling to risk personal embarrassment.

As you might imagine, I did not pass out. Nor did any of the other fears materialize. In fact, an old childhood friend came back to Christ that night. We had attended that church together as children and she, too, had allowed the years to crowd Christ out of her life. God had demonstrated to me that night that He is sufficient to conquer the monster of all monsters—the human ego!

In Sunday School recently, we were discussing God's chain-of-command. If you want to upset people, just mention two words—**authority** and **submission.** Yet Christianity is based on those two words. They are life-sustaining principles that keep our lives in proper relation to our Savior. One cannot become a Christian without **submitting** his will to Christ. One cannot **grow** as a Christian without accepting God's final **authority** over his life. But even in the Christian life, there is usually a real tug-of-war between God's will and self-will.

I used to blame Eve for the mess I was in, until I realized I was willfully biting into my own apples of selfishness. For awhile it tasted pretty good! I thought I knew what would make me happy. I thought I had the answers for my life. Like Eve, I soon began to choke on the seeds of my own destruction.

Submitting my will to God was the first step. It was then I learned how to love myself and others in the proper order. Abiding by His authority continues to be a daily process of dying to self.

For when you are deadened to sin you are freed from all
its allure and its power over you. And since your old
sin-loving nature "died" with Christ, we know that you will
share his new life (Rom. 6:7-8, TLB).

All of life looks so different now. As I am learning
to see with God's unlimited vision, there is beauty in
the most unexpected places. There are opportunities
to love and forgive that I had never noticed before.
And there is joy as I bury the old Cyvette and rise to
"share His new life."

# LIFELINES

**On days when the big NUMBER ONE gets in the way of others, find guidance in these words:**

☆

Search me, O God, and know my heart; test my thoughts. Point out anything you find in me that makes you sad, and lead me along the path of everlasting life (Ps. 139:23-24, TLB).

☆

Don't think only of yourself. Try to think of the other fellow, too, and what is best for him (1 Cor. 10:24, TLB).

☆

He died for all so that all who live—having received eternal life from him—might live no longer for themselves, to please themselves, but to spend their lives pleasing Christ who died and rose again for them (2 Cor. 5:15, TLB).

☆

Don't just think about your own affairs, but be interested in others, too, and in what they are doing (Phil. 2:4, TLB).

☆

Yes indeed, it is good when you truly obey our Lord's command, "You must love and help your neighbors just as much as you love and take care of yourself" (Jas. 2:8, TLB).

# Chapter 7

# The Way the Ball Bounces
## (Circumstances)

My non-Christian days were spent in the "woe is me" syndrome. Life, it seemed, was to be endured, but certainly not enjoyed. That attitude carried over even after my conversion. I was in such a habit of making a "big deal" out of my problems and circumstances, it was difficult to change.

I spent the first two years of my Christian life allowing my health to rob me of the continuing joy of being a Christian. After the birth of our third son, my pancreas would not function properly. I was told by the doctors that if the condition did not correct itself, there was nothing they could do to help me. The pancreas is as vital as the heart. One cannot live if it fails to function.

I could not remember what it was like to wake up in the morning with renewed strength to begin the day. I felt so weak and trembly that even the thought of cooking breakfast was overwhelming. Depression moved in like a great weight that drained my already depleted resources.

Oh, how I prayed, begged, bargained, and pleaded with God to heal me! Fellow believers who were concerned about my health offered many suggestions as to how I should pray. When I didn't receive any apparent results, these well-intended suggestions simply added to my frustration. Was God deaf? Didn't He care? Didn't He mean it when He said to ask "anything" in His name, believing, and it would be done? (Matt. 21:22). There was but one obvious conclusion to my dilemma, I reasoned. I simply didn't have enough faith. The problem could not be with God, so it had to be my fault.

At the time, we were still living in St. Petersburg. Each Sunday morning during prayer, our minister would say, "Lord Jesus, touch the one here today with the greatest need—the one who needs you the most." I always felt that "one" was me. Surely no one sitting in those pews could have been more disillusioned with life, more drained, more in need of the Master's touch. For me, Jesus was my last hope. If He could not bring some purpose and meaning into my life, then there was nowhere else to turn.

One desperate night, I decided to forget myself and my illness. Irritated with God's apparent indifference, I told a close friend I was tired of praying for healing and that I would not mention it to God again. I would just be the best servant I could be **under the circumstances.** Behind those words hid much anger and disillusionment with God.

But in spite of those angry feelings, strange things began to happen. As a result of my reluctant surrender, I discovered that I **could be joyful in the Lord whether sick or well!**

As Christians, our circumstances should not dictate our joy! That principle was the opposite of all I had ever known. I had learned, in a small measure, the truth of Paul's teaching from Philippians.

For I have learned, in whatever state I am, to be content. I know how to be abased, and I know how to abound; in any and all circumstances I have learned the secret of facing plenty and hunger, abundance and want. I can do all things in him who strengthens me (Phil. 4:11-13, RSV).

As I clung to that passage, I realized one day I was not shaking or having to eat every hour. Then, much to my surprise, I could make it past lunchtime without being on the verge of passing out. I couldn't thank God enough.

I have experienced the burden of serving God under affliction, and I am thankful He removed it from me. But I am more thankful that He first taught me His grace is sufficient "in any and all circumstances."

If you are ill at this moment and feel God is not hearing you, then consider this suggestion. In order to be healed, you must first be willing **not to be.** The answer to suffering is not a prayer lifted between teeth gritted in determination. Nor can you ask conditionally: "**If** you'll heal me, Lord, I'll be a better Christian." I tried that one many times. God responds to the obedient and submissive heart.

Many times I have heard evangelists say that if someone is not healed, it is because his faith is not strong enough. What an additional and unscriptural burden to place on the one who is suffering! To take this viewpoint is to ignore scripture that clearly teaches suffering. Christ Himself suffered because there was work to be done in the suffering.

I believe with all my heart that God longs for all of us to be whole—physically and spiritually. I also know that at times He will sacrifice our physical comfort for the growth of the spiritual body.

My middle son recently had one of those "growth" experiences. Thad took a bad fall on his bicycle and broke his jaw. He had to enter the hospital to have his mouth wired shut. The healing process was expected to take at least six weeks. When the doctors first clamped his mouth shut, I thought Thad would die! (If you really want to identify, try clamping your teeth together and imagine leaving them that way for six weeks.) He wanted to hit something—anything. He felt that he was going to suffocate. Tears of frustration rolled down his cheeks. Hours passed as he fought a real battle with himself. Crying only made his nose stuffy and added to the "smothery" feeling. I really began to pray for him as I attempted to comfort him as best I could.

By the next morning, I saw a marked change. Instead of defiance and belligerance, I saw acceptance and surrender. Thad seemed to understand that all the fighting, complaining, and crying in the world would not solve his problem. It was something to be endured as patiently as possible.

Thad could have blamed God for his circumstances. Instead, he chose to draw from God's storehouse of resources and simply accept what had happened. He got on with living and the six weeks passed quickly.

When Gene and I first became Christians, our joy was determined by the balance in our checking account. If there was money in the bank, we were happy. If we had to count pennies, we were unhappy. What a fickle commodity on which to hinge happiness! God took us through many a financial squeeze before we learned to be joyful **in the midst of them.**

I love the way God always provides opportunities for me to practice what I preach. When I heard we were moving to Paint Lick, I knew that it had to be a rural community when I couldn't find it on the map! That also meant the parsonage would probably be quite a bit different from the modern home I was leaving behind. So, if there was no indoor plumbing, I would simply put ruffly curtains in the little house out back and fluffy padding on the seat! With a determined heart, I turned all my apprehensions over to God and resolved to be grateful for whatever conditions we found.

But when we rounded the final bend approaching the parsonage, my resolution failed me. High atop a hill stood a forlorn-looking white frame house, badly in need of a face-lifting. Right next to it was the garage, the door hanging by one rusty hinge.

We approached the parsonage with misgivings. Once inside, the musty smell of "old" confirmed my worst fears. The bathroom was not an outhouse, but close to it! In front of the tub was a huge, gaping hole that dropped into the basement below. Spiders had taken up housekeeping in all the ancient plumbing fixtures. So what did I do? I ran outside, sat down under a big oak tree, and cried. After I finished my cry, I had a little talk with myself and decided I had a choice to make. I could be miserable and continue to compare the parsonage with our lovely house with a pool in Florida, or I could accept it and busy myself making it a real home.

Across the street quietly stood the little church my husband had come to pastor. It seemed to breathe its own benediction—the promise of better things to come. I dried my eyes and picked up the broom.

Life is full of surprises and disappointments. Cars are always breaking down, clothes need mending, teeth need filling, lawn mowers quit mowing, and on and on. Sometimes it seems that only God is still working! Often these very circumstances are the tools He uses to hone us into His "peculiar people."

Circumstances should not affect our joy level. We can learn to live above them, just as Paul did . . .

> I have worked harder, been put in jail oftener, been whipped times without number, and faced death again and again and again. Five different times the Jews gave me their thirty-nine lashes. Three times I was shipwrecked. Once I was in the open sea all night and the whole next day. I have traveled many weary miles and have been often in great danger from flooded rivers, and from robbers, and from my own people, the Jews, as well as from the hands of the Gentiles. I have faced grave dangers from mobs in the cities and from death in the deserts and in the stormy seas and from men who claim to be brothers in Christ but are not. I have lived with weariness and pain and sleepless nights. Often I have been hungry and thirsty and have gone without food; often I have shivered with cold, without enough clothing to keep me warm (2 Cor. 11:23-27, TLB).

That awesome list leaves me feeling a bit foolish and somewhat ashamed. I haven't been beaten lately, no shipwrecks or floods or mob scenes. I don't always get all I **want** to eat, but more than I **need.** If ever anyone had reason to complain of his circumstances, certainly Paul did. But listen to his words:

> Since I know it is all for Christ's good, I am quite happy . . . about insults and hardships, persecutions and difficulties; for when I am weak, then I am strong—the less I have, the more I depend on him (2 Cor. 12:10, TLB).

Paul's attitude toward troublesome circumstances was to be "quite happy"! Impossible? Not when our Source of happiness is Christ. Paul explained,

> I want you to know this, dear brothers: Everything that has happened to me here has been a great boost in getting out the Good News concerning Christ (Phil. 1:12, TLB).

Using this verse as his text, Dr. J. P. Allen, a well-known pastor from Ft. Worth, Texas, preached a sermon entitled "WHAT HAPPENS TO WHAT HAPPENS TO YOU?" He concluded that though "we cannot control what happens to us, we can control **what happens** to what happens to us!"

We can rise above our circumstances by incorporating actively the power of Jesus Christ into our lives. The joy that He gives is not so fragile that it can be destroyed by outward trials and conditions. God's gifts to us are totally indestructible. Christ said:

> "I am leaving you with a gift—peace of mind and heart! And the peace I give isn't fragile like the peace the world gives. So don't be troubled or afraid" (John 14:27, TLB).

The kind of peace that Christ is speaking of is not that which accompanies riches or good health, only to vanish when the stock market crashes or the body fails. The Christian's peace and joy are able to withstand all the storms that may come.

> Do not rejoice against me, O my enemy, for though I fall, I will rise again! When I sit in darkness, the Lord himself will be my Light (Micah 7:8, TLB).

I will rise again and so will you. Circumstances are the fragile things of life. They will pass away, but the joy of the Lord will endure forever!

# LIFELINES

**Some precious promises for days when every-thing goes wrong . . .**

☆

Those who sow tears shall reap joy. Yes, they go out weeping, carrying seed for sowing, and return singing, carrying their sheaves (Ps. 126:5-6, TLB).

☆

Fear not, for I am with you. Do not be dismayed. I am your God. I will strengthen you; I will help you; I will uphold you with my victorious right hand (Isa. 41:10, TLB).

☆

We can rejoice, too, when we run into problems and trials for we know that they are good for us . . . and help us trust God more each time . . . until our hope and faith are strong and steady (Rom. 5:3, TLB).

☆

We are pressed on every side by troubles, but not crushed and broken. We are perplexed because we don't know why things happen as they do, but we don't give up and quit . . . God never abandons us (2 Cor. 4:8-9, TLB).

☆

Whatever happens, Dear friends, be glad in the Lord (Phil. 3:1, TLB).

☆

Let him have all your worries and cares, for he is always thinking about you and watching everything that concerns you (1 Pet. 5:7, TLB).

# Chapter 8

# Bitter Roots

## (Bitterness)

Bitterness and joy cannot row in the same boat. If one climbs in, there is no room for the other. Bitterness is a poor substitute for joy!

Several years ago my older sister, Neva, had a dispute with a friend that left a bitter taste for months afterward. She prayed many times that it be removed. It would disappear for awhile only to crop up again.

After struggling with the problem for some time, she and her husband, Joe, took a trip to the Holy Land. She prayed that on the trip God would permanently remove the bitterness from her heart.

One of the places they visited was the tomb of Jesus. As Neva entered the tomb, she found herself separated from the group. Standing in an alcove of the cave, she prayed once again that God would remove the bitterness. Suddenly she saw a vision. On the empty slab where Jesus had once lain appeared a figure. It was the body of Jesus, bleeding from the side. Nail prints were visible in his hands and feet. She heard Him say, "Neva, when they laid me in this tomb, I had already forgiven my persecutors. If anyone had a right to feel betrayed, it was I."

In an instant she was delivered from her bitterness. The dramatic encounter completely changed her perspective.

Yet many times we are content to cling to our bitterness. Feeling the offending party deserves our wrath, we play the game of grudges. Our life begins to revolve around how to get even. The offense grows in our minds until it is bigger than we are!

> Watch out that no bitterness takes root among you, for as it springs up it causes deep trouble, hurting many in their spiritual lives (Heb. 12:15, TLB).

Bitterness is no respecter of persons. No one is immune. It is like an insidious poison that can infiltrate the lifestream of any believer or nonbeliever at any stage of life.

Not long ago, I conducted some workshops at a weekend retreat. My topic was "bitterness." Many of the women who attended were college girls. When I saw them, I almost panicked. "Lord," I cried, "these girls can't know anything about bitterness. They haven't lived long enough. Did I understand you correctly when you told me how to prepare?"

He answered, "Trust Me."

I guess I don't have to tell you what happened that weekend. Pent-up emotions spilled over. Dark secrets were shared. There were heartbreaking stories of parents who didn't know how to communicate, in-laws who had never accepted the marriage, roommates who had betrayed confidences, husbands and boyfriends who had strayed. Healing tears fell as God began to excise these roots of bitterness from some tender, young hearts.

These malignant roots, if left to spread, might have eventually choked all future relationships and produced other unhealthy outgrowths.

In a seminar on "Basic Youth Conflicts" conducted by Bill Gothard, I learned that one of the consequences of bitterness is depression. It requires a great deal of emotional energy to hold a grudge. As we maintain our bitterness, we deplete our energy store, leaving none for the other dilemmas of daily living.

Depression has assumed epidemic proportions. As a Christian, I believe in the ability of the human mind to endure extreme stress. I believe that because I believe in the wisdom of the One who created man. If an engineer can design a suspension bridge to withstand tons and tons of weight and pressure, surely God's engineering is vastly superior. However, in our willful way, we have insisted on throwing wrenches into the machinery. One of those wrenches is bitterness.

When we harbor bitterness, we become slaves to the objects of our bitterness. Those persons dominate our thoughts. They rob us of our energy. They cause our bodies to go haywire, producing ulcers and headaches and even heart attacks! We want to hurt those who have hurt us, and instead, they destroy us without lifting a finger.

When we harbor bitterness, we are refusing to acknowledge the fact that we could be partly responsible for the breach. Perhaps someone has simply found one of our sensitive areas. Perhaps God is using that person to point out a character flaw. Whatever the reason, God can use the offending party to develop our characters more fully.

The supreme consequence of bitterness is an inability to forgive—creating a gulf between ourselves and God. In his seminar Bill Gothard said that we often pray glibly and carelessly the beautiful Lord's Prayer. One section in particular makes hypocrites of many of us. "Forgive us our trespasses as we forgive those who trespass against us." If we are guilty of an unforgiving spirit, our very words condemn us.

It was not until my sister gave up her grudge that she was able to examine her own part in the situation. In all honesty she had to admit that she must share the blame.

Moreover, she learned that when someone wrongs a Christian, it is then the **Christian's** opportunity and responsibility to be the first to forgive!

> Therefore if thou bring thy gift to the altar, and there rememberest that thy brother hath aught against thee; Leave there thy gift before the altar, and go thy way; first be reconciled to thy brother, and then come and offer thy gift (Matt. 5:23-24).

"First, be reconciled to thy brother!" is a commandment, not a suggestion. If we could look at **offenses** as special **God-given opportunities**, we would never have to deal with bitterness again.

The Apostle Paul was able to witness many times to his jailers because he held no malice toward any man. He looked at his prison terms as "opportunities." He was never bitter toward his persecutors because he was too busy looking beyond their **deeds** to discover their **needs.**

One basic need that is shared by every human being is the need for love. The most bitter and ingrown people I know have been those who have never known love. Some things in life can best be understood through experience. Love is like that. Words may only get in the way. The most beautiful words in the English language, **I love you,** do not mean very much if they are not supported by loving actions.

When we lived in St. Petersburg, our neighborhood was full of children who needed love. There were many working parents whose children were left unattended all day. Other parents didn't seem to care when their children came or went. There were other families with "his" and "hers" living under the same roof, trying to adjust to the merger created by remarriage. Our home, centered around the love of Christ, seemed to act as a magnet for these neighborhood "orphans."

Consequently, our front yard always looked like the city playground. Sometimes Gene and I would become irritated over our dying grass. I mentioned the problem one day to our pastor's wife. She said something I've never forgotten: "Cyvette, grass will grow again. Those children have but one chance. You may be that chance." Why hadn't I thought of that?! Of course I wanted them to see Christ in me. But all they had been seeing was a frazzled housewife with a sign that plainly read, "Keep Off the Grass," and in fine print, "and out of my life!" God had planted me in that neighborhood for a purpose. I set about immediately to mend my fences—or, better still, to tear them down altogether!

I decided to begin a children's Bible study. The boys passed the word at school that we would be meeting every Thursday afternoon—and there would be plenty of refreshments! I knew that it would take time before the children could develop an appetite for Bible study—the snacks would ensure their return. But I soon found that they were just as hungry for the Word!

That first Thursday, our house was full of wide-eyed kids. They lined the living room, expectant and eager to hear what this was all about. At that moment I prayed, "Oh, God, I'm not big enough for this job!" He replied, "I am."

My "students" and I had a great time with God's Word that afternoon and many others to follow. Before moving to Kentucky, I made it my goal to share the plan of salvation with every child in the group. That gave me exactly one year.

It was a busy year, filled with fun and new friendships—and a steady diet of love. We called ourselves the "Royal Crusaders," and each child tried to live up to that name. You could hear them in the front yard after Bible study checking each other on cursing, lying, and dishonest play.

Just four years before, I would have bitterly resented the type of children who lived in my neighborhood. My blood would have boiled at the thought of negligent parents. My tongue would have lashed the irresponsible kids running through my yard and ruining my grass. But because of the new love of Christ in my heart, I could see the emptiness in their lives. It broke my heart and spurred me to an action that I have never regretted.

> Take care to live in me, and let me live in you. For a branch can't produce fruit when severed from the vine. Nor can you be fruitful apart from me . . . I have told you this so that you will be filled with my joy (John 15:4, 11, TLB).

I pray that the seeds that were planted that year have produced lasting fruit and that the roots have grown deep and strong in the love of God.

# LIFELINES

**The only way to uproot bitterness is to plant these living words in your heart.**

☆

Your heavenly Father will forgive you if you forgive those who sin against you; but if you refuse to forgive them, he will not forgive you (Matt. 6:14-15, TLB).

☆

But when you are praying, first forgive anyone you are holding a grudge against, so that your Father in Heaven will forgive you your sins (Mark 11:25, TLB).

☆

"Rebuke your brother if he sins and forgive him if he is sorry. Even if he wrongs you several times a day and each time turns again and asks forgiveness, forgive him."(Luke 17:3-4, TLB).

☆

Be gentle and ready to forgive; never hold grudges. Remember, the Lord forgave you, so you must forgive others (Col. 3:13, TLB).

# Chapter 9

# All That Glitters . . .
## (Worldliness)

This world is not our home, but I do admire the tasteful furnishings selected by its Designer— majestic mountains, star-spangled heavens, carpets of lush green grass and vast sandy deserts, wide stretches of ocean, ribbons of rivers illuminated by great glowing light fixtures in the sky. And then God created man to inhabit His world. That's when all the trouble began. Man forgot that he was only a guest on planet earth and began to exploit its resources.

Now, centuries later, the picture is dismal indeed. Man has assumed squatter's rights to the land, established a technological society, and has set about to produce and accumulate for himself more and more possessions. Materialism has become a major joy robber for Christians who are striving to be "in the world, but not of it."

I'll admit that I have a problem at this point. I enjoy many things this world has to offer. I enjoy watching a crackling fire on a cold winter's night, but fireplaces cost money. I enjoy having dinner with friends, but food is expensive. I enjoy a Gaither concert, but it costs $22.00 for our entire family to attend.

Are these possessions and pleasures "worldly"? How can we justify them when so much of the world is in need? Is there some valid scale of values for committed Christians?

I can remember thinking that Christianity and poverty were usually mentioned in the same breath. A Christian was automatically poor—rattletrap car, hand-me-down clothes, grits and beans. That's hardly an appealing picture, is it?

Then we read in the Old Testament how the kings lived in lavish surroundings. A description of King Solomon's palace makes one wonder why God allowed such luxury, especially when we read in the New Testament that it is more difficult for a rich man to enter into the kingdom of heaven than it is for a camel to pass through the eye of a needle.

Perhaps it would help to clarify some terms used in the Bible. There are two words describing a person with many possessions—**rich** and **wealthy.** In the Bible a "rich" man is one with many material possessions but without "spiritual heritage." He has money and money has him. It is his god.

A "very" rich ruler came to Jesus and asked, "Good Master, what must I do to inherit eternal life?"

> Jesus said to him, "Sell all that thou hast, and distribute unto the poor, and thou shalt have treasure in heaven; and come, follow me" (Luke 18:22).

The rich man hung his head, signaling defeat, and walked away from the offer of a lifetime. He preferred to keep all he had, things that would eventually rust, decay, and become moth-eaten—than to accept an invitation to the nontarnishable treasures of heaven.

A modern-day version of this story is the man who approached a friend and said, "I hear you are in great danger. I understand that you are getting rich!"

I worked in the medical records department of a large university hospital. One night I came across the records of a millionaire who was hospitalized on the verge of a nervous breakdown. The psychological data was extensive. As I read, the sad story unfolded of a man who had tried to buy happiness and then lost his son. When this tragedy struck, his world literally fell in around him. No amount of money could bring back his son; his vast fortune was totally worthless. Until that tragedy, he had been able to manage his life well—money had always bought the answers.

"You cannot serve two masters; God and money. For you will hate one and love the other; or else the other way around" (Matt. 6:24, TLB).

The man whose master is money accumulates possessions for his own use. He enjoys the position and respect often associated with money. He is always looking for ways to get more. His "giving" is usually tax-deductible and offered for the purpose of improving his image or easing his conscience. He never gives sacrificially but comfortably and with piety, expecting others to appreciate his generosity.

A **wealthy** man, as frequently defined by the Scriptures, is one who realizes that his possessions are of "divine ownership." In essence, this man is investing God's capital in ways which will further the work of the Kingdom. He is not "getting" for himself, but rather "accepts" gifts from God, realizing he may be called upon to give them away!

And thou say in thine heart, My power and the might of mine hand hath gotten me this wealth. But thou shalt remember the Lord thy God: for it is he that giveth thee power to get wealth, that he may establish his covenant which he sware unto thy fathers, as it is this day (Deut. 8:17-18).

Therefore, God is asking us to be good stewards of our material possessions—to be willing to give them up or to share them. Placing more value on **things** than on our relationship to God is a powerful joy robber.

Most of us are not millionaires. We are the average family, trying to meet the obligations of a demanding economy. If you want to discover how demanding the economy is, you should experience a salary reduction from $1,400 a month to $400. That was our experience when Gene began his studies for the ministry.

After moving to Kentucky, I began the clothing shop, hoping to supplement the family income while Gene was in school. The idea that **God** could really meet our needs wasn't one of the options we considered! I almost worked myself to death before I collapsed and cried out, "God, what are you trying to tell me!" The answer was so simple. "Let **Me** provide for your needs. You stay home and take care of the children. You cheer Gene up when he comes dragging in at night, his mind exploding with Greek. You clean the house and keep things orderly for your husband, and I'll worry about your needs!" Well, God didn't use quite those words, but after a period of time, all those things added up. I put the shop up for sale and we began to live by faith—with two car payments, insurance, food, clothing, medical expenses to pay—excuse me—for God to pay.

Several weeks later, the church increased Gene's salary by thirty-three percent. We were amazed! That increase greatly helped, but there were still many times God had to make manna fall from heaven on our behalf. How exciting to stand on a promise and watch Him keep that promise!

Therefore I say unto you, take no thought for your life, what ye shall eat or what ye shall drink; nor yet for your body, what ye shall put on . . . for your heavenly Father knoweth that ye have need of all these things. But seek ye first the kingdom of God, and his righteousness; and all these things shall be added unto you (Matt. 6:25, 32-33).

I will **never** again do anything just for the money! My life's work is a "calling,"directed by God and channeled through Him for approval.

However, I have come to the conclusion that my love for money will be a continuing battle. I conquer the problem only to battle it again. I win the battle during the "lean" times and find myself slipping during the plentiful times. We are in the greatest danger of experiencing "worldliness" when God has bountifully blessed! In the words of Dwight L. Moody, "We can stand affliction better than we can prosperity, for in prosperity we forget God."

Therefore, I am learning with Paul,

In whatsoever state I am, therewith to be content (Phil. 4:11).

Men with great riches have offered to trade all their money for the secret of immortality. God has been offering that secret to men **free** for over 2,000 years. It makes one wonder why there aren't more takers!

# LIFELINES

This world is not our permanent home; it is passing away. Keep things in perspective with these assurances from God's Word.

☆

What profit is there if you gain the whole world—and lose eternal life? What can be compared with the value of eternal life (Matt. 16:26, TLB)?

☆

Don't copy the behavior and customs of this world, but be a new and different person with a fresh newness in all you do and think. Then you will learn from your own experience how his ways will really satisfy you (Rom. 12:2, TLB).

☆

Those in frequent contact with the exciting things the world offers should make good use of their opportunities without stopping to enjoy them; for the world in its present form will soon be gone (1 Cor. 7:31, TLB).

☆

God wants us to turn from our godless living and sinful pleasures and to live good, God-fearing lives day after day (Titus 2:12, TLB).

☆

Stop loving this evil world and all that it offers you, for when you love these things you show that you do not really love God (1 John 2:15, TLB).

# Chapter 10

# First Things First
## (Priorities)

Some days I get so uptight I could literally explode. I feel put out, misunderstood, overworked, disorganized, unappreciated, unspiritual, incompetent, and totally miserable. As a Christian, I wish I could always be serene, contented, controlled, and on top of things. But when the going gets rough, I usually take it out on those nearest and dearest. I can empty the house in a matter of seconds when that black mood descends upon me.

I hate myself when I turn into this stranger who can't cope. But, thank the Lord, I have found a solution. I have been blessed with a husband who is as solid as a rock, and I really lean on him when Mama turns monster. I rant and rave till I run out of energy. Then, like a whipped puppy, I run to him in tears, asking, "Gene, what is wrong with me? I am miserable and I'm making everyone else miserable."

He has a pretty standard response to that question, "Cyvette, you've got your priorities out of order again." Always, the truth of that simple statement hits me with such force that I am overwhelmed by the fact that such an obvious conclusion could have escaped me.

As you can see, the proper ordering of priorities has been a continuing battle for me. Like most Christians, I love life, and there just aren't enough hours in the day to cover everything I would like to do. But I try anyway! Therein lies the problem. I tend to run from one project to the next before completing the first!

A perfect example of misplaced priorities is my writing. When I really get involved with a book, the house could fall in around me and I'd never notice unless a board hit me directly on the head. When the kids ask me something during those creative times, I answer with a halting "Uh-huh—what'd you say? Yeah, I guess so, go ahead," and continue to type. They know I am not really hearing them, and they have taken advantage of that situation more than once. The house slowly deteriorates—washing piles up; floors go unmopped; carpets collect dust; clutter gathers in the corners; and husband gets uptight over the whole situation. When I do finally snap out of it or hit a snag in my writing, I cannot believe the condition of the house! I become instantly and completely strung out. It doesn't matter if I do think that I have written a chapter that will change the world, I am now torn between responsibilities.

While reading God's Word one night, I was intrigued with the scripture that warns against dividing our minds. That scripture says,

> Every kingdom divided against itself is brought to desolation; and a house divided against a house falleth (Luke 11:17).

That verse clearly described my condition! You can't have ten projects going all at once and not expect to pay the price. I discovered that I could destroy the house of my mind by dividing my mental and emotional focus over an extended period of time.

When I first began to sell my writing, I thought, "Wow, this is **really** important! God has called me to be a Christian writer." I forgot for a little while that He had **first** called me to be a wife and mother. While in this lapse of memory, I wrote and wrote. The more I wrote, the more unhappy I became.

God began to nudge me to reaffirm the priorities He had already given me. Next to my own spiritual growth, my foremost responsibility is to meet the needs of the family that God has entrusted to me. Even if I become a best-selling author, I will not resign my role as "maker-of-the-home."

Today's variety of life-styles beckons us in many enticing directions. Women especially fight this battle, pulled between full-time work or full-time motherhood. Many are choosing the outside job, giving their best hours to their employers and thereby serving their families with leftover energies.

I really came under conviction about priorities when I began my used clothing store. I discovered that it takes a great deal of emotional, mental, and physical energy to run a business—even a small one. Just filling out the forms sent by the government is enough to make anybody cry "uncle"! By the time four o'clock came around each day, I had nothing left to give to my family waiting at home. They almost dreaded seeing me in the afternoons. Was I smiling? Never! Patient? Hardly! I was burning the candle at both ends and quickly running out of wick. This miserable set of circumstances continued for almost a year.

To complicate things Bobby John was then only four, so I had to arrange for someone to take care of him. I found a lovely Christian lady whose house was conveniently located on my way to work. But Bobby John had something against her—she wasn't his mother. Every morning we would play the same scene—Bobby John hanging on to the car bumper while I tried to disengage him so I could carry him into the sitter's house. I lectured and scolded him for being so possessive, urging him to be a "big boy!" How foolish! I should have been thrilled that he wanted to stay with me. But I cruelly shoved him off on someone else so that I could go and make a dollar. I convinced myself that it was time he learned to do without me every minute. I certainly would not give in to his tantrums!

That line of reasoning sounded pretty good. I had heard countless other mothers use it successfully, but it simply wasn't working for me. The Spirit faithfully continued to remind me that Bobby John was my responsibility—not the babysitter's. No one else could give him **my** love; I should not pay someone else to do the job I should be doing. "Cyvette," the Spirit gently chided, "is the money you are making worth what it is costing your small son?"

Then one memorable Sunday, my husband preached a sermon on priorities. "If we honor our priorities," he said, "God will meet our needs." When we got home from church, I had a surprise announcement. "Gene," I said, "I want to sell the shop. I realize that I have my priorities out of order. You helped me see that this morning."

After much discussion, we realized that God had indeed spoken to us through Gene's sermon. The shop was sold in just a few months, and once again I was a full-time wife and mother. Order and a sense of well-being returned to our home.

I made all sorts of promises to myself that I would give Gene and the boys my best efforts. I would clean out all those cluttered drawers and bulging closets. I would be superwife and supermom. For awhile I kept my resolution. Then adventure called via the typewriter, and once again I was a part-time homemaker. Did you know you can actually be at home twenty-four hours a day and still be "away"?

Priorities, then, are only honored properly when we give them our best. There will be no honor before God for the sloppy, unimaginative, bored housewives who are just serving their time. God will not be giving out crowns to pastors who didn't take seriously their calling or husbands who refused to become the heads of their families. We won't get a gold star for just enduring with a stiff upper lip!

Gradually, I began to experience real and total fulfillment in my ministry as a housewife and mother. Though I have outside interests, I simply will not allow anything to demand more from me than I am able to give. I still write, perhaps more fruitfully than ever, but only after I have taken care of my first priority. It is a challenge to accomplish my main tasks of the day so that I can sit down to my typewriter with a clear conscience.

Some weeks ago a job opportunity presented itself. It sounded like the perfect job and, since Bobby John is now in the first grade, I seriously considered accepting it. I approached my husband with the job offer. He vetoed the idea emphatically. He said that he couldn't stand the thought of the way things used to be. I knew what he meant by that remark! Strangely enough, my "freedom" was not threatened at all. Actually, when he said no, I was elated. I knew I had made myself count as a housewife and mother. To Gene, I was too valuable an asset to trade for mere money!

How can we know when we have our priorities out of order? The first signal is confusion. God is not the author of confusion, but of supreme order! When things begin piling up or become too difficult to handle, perhaps energies are being invested amiss. We have a limited amount of energy to expend; and when it's depleted, there is no more. When we constantly overextend ourselves, depression and extreme fatigue will inevitably result.

Another signal that priorities are out of order is nonproductive praying. God is not going to provide us with more energy when we are investing that energy contrary to His perfect will. Many times I have had to call on His strength when mine ran out. I always receive it when I am in His will. But when that power doesn't flow, then I must ask myself what's wrong!

So often we have the best of intentions. I see this pattern especially in those who are eager to serve the Lord. Before long, they find themselves wearing too many hats—youth director, Sunday School teacher, choir member, evangelistic leader, and church bus driver! That's what I call dividing oneself! Surely God would rather have us invest ourselves completely and effectively in one or two projects rather than attacking them all ineffectively.

> Each man's work will become manifest (obvious); for the Day will disclose it . . . and the fire will test what sort of work each one has done. If the work which any man has built on the foundation survives, he will receive a reward (1 Cor. 3:13-14, RSV).

God obviously isn't going to be passing out rewards for "busy work," but for that work which bears fruit! Beware of priority pirates disguised as missions of mercy. As Grandma used to say, "Don't put so many irons on the coals that you make the fire go out."

# LIFELINES

**When there is just too much to do, too little time, no one to help—turn your eyes upon Jesus:**

☆

In everything you do, put God first, and he will direct you and crown your efforts with success (Prov. 3:6, TLB).

☆

"So don't worry at all about having enough food and clothing. Why be like the heathen? For they take pride in all these things and are deeply concerned about them. But your heavenly Father already knows perfectly well that you need them, and he will give them to you if you give him first place in your life and live as he wants you to" (Matt. 6:31-33. TLB).

☆

Be sure that everything is done properly in a good and orderly way (1 Cor. 14:40, TLB).

☆

Best of all, they went beyond our highest hopes, for their first action was to dedicate themselves to the Lord and to us, for whatever directions God might give to them through us (2 Cor. 8:5, TLB).

☆

This should be your ambition: to live a quiet life, minding your own business and doing your own work (1 Thess. 4:11, TLB).

# Part Two
# The Joy Givers

# Chapter 11

# The Counselor

While I was still a young Christian, my pastor preached a sermon on the Holy Spirit. I knew that my Christian experience was lacking in power. I just didn't seem to have what it took to accomplish anything worthwhile for the Kingdom. I longed to be a constant Christian—one who could be counted on daily, in ordinary ways. That takes a power of even a deeper kind. So when I heard my pastor saying that this power was available to me for the asking, I couldn't **wait** to get to the altar to receive it. The moment the invitation was given, I went! I was trying to avoid the rush. Yet of the large number of people who heard that sermon, I was the only one who went forward. There was no stampede for the altar as I had expected. Alone, I knelt at the long altar rail with 400 pairs of eyes staring at me! But I didn't care. I wanted what Christ had died to give me and I received it that day just for the asking! My life has never been the same. Finally, something was worth more to me than my own goals and ambitions. I found that, like the disciples in the Bible, I was willing and even eager to pay whatever price is necessary to follow Jesus.

If I could write with the skill of a C. S. Lewis or a Catherine Marshall or Paul, the words describing the changes in my life would leap from this page and set your heart on fire. And if I could sit down with you and share all day and all night, I would need still more time to relate all that these changes have meant. I only know what life was like before I received Christ and the power of His Holy Spirit and I don't want to go back! The old life was full of Cyvette and what she wanted. The new life is full of Jesus and what He wants. I have been taught by that faithful Spirit to lose my life so that I could truly find it. For as it says in Galatians 2:20, TLB:

> I have been crucified with Christ; and I myself no longer live, but Christ lives in me. And the real life I now have within this body is a result of my trusting in the Son of God, who loved me and gave himself for me.

One of the most enlightening stories I have ever read on the matter of the Holy Spirit was told of Dr. Walter Wilson, who lived in the early 1900's and founded many ministries, including Kansas City Bible College. This man, up until his encounter with the Holy Spirit, had had a relatively fruitless ministry. His enthusiasm for the Lord was abundant, but his power was pathetically nil. This lack of fruitfulness had become a thorn in his side, and he shared his dilemma with a trusted friend. After listening intently to Dr. Wilson's story, the friend asked him, "What is the Holy Spirit to you?" Wilson's answer was, "He is one of the Persons of the Godhead . . . a Teacher, a Guide, third Person of the Trinity."

To this his friend carefully pointed out that he had given the Holy Spirit a place of insignificance and inferiority, stating, "He is just as great, just as precious, just as needful as the other two Persons of the Trinity. But still you have not answered my question. What is He to **you**?"

To this Wilson truthfully replied, "He is nothing to me. I have no contact with Him, no personal relationship, and could get along quite well without Him."

Dr. Wilson's friend was grieved by the honest answer given and replied, "Then that is why your life is so fruitless, even though your efforts are great. If you will seek personally to know the Holy Spirit, He will transform your life."

Many events followed that brought Dr. Wilson closer and closer to accepting this truth. The culminating event took place one night when he went to hear a message given by Dr. James M. Gray, who was later to become the president of Moody Bible Institute. That message so inspired and enlightened Dr. Wilson that he could not deny the truth any longer. Immediately after the services, he went directly home. Utterly heartbroken over his fruitless life, he had within him a new hope. He lay upon the carpet of his study, prostrate in God's presence. The following are the words he spoke: "There, in the quiet of that late hour, I said to the Holy Spirit, 'My Lord, I have mistreated You all my Christian life. I have treated You like a servant. When I wanted You, I called for You; when I was about to engage in some work, I beckoned You to come and help me perform my task. I have kept You in the place of a servant. I have sought to use You only as a willing servant to help me in my self-appointed and chosen work. I shall do so no more. Just now I give You this body of mine; from my head to my feet, I give it to You. I give You my hands, my limbs, my eyes and lips, my brain; all that I am within and without, I hand over to You for You to live in it the life that You please. You may send this body to

Africa or lay it on a bed with cancer. You may blind the eyes or send me with your message to Tibet. You may take this body to the Eskimos or send it to a hospital with pneumonia. It is Your body from this moment on. Help Yourself to it. Thank You, My Lord, I believe You have accepted it, for in Romans 12:1 You said "acceptable unto God." Thank you again, my Lord, for taking me. We now belong to each other.' "

The results that followed were staggering! He no longer had a fruitless ministry but one that radiated with the very Spirit of the living Lord!

Perhaps the question we should ask ourselves is not how much of the Holy Spirit do we have, but rather how much of us does the Holy Spirit have?

Our churches are filled with Christians who are struggling to live in their own strength. Little wonder that they are defeated daily by fear, anxiety, compromise, guilt, etc. Their Christian experience is nothing more than a battle fought with a dull sword against a powerful adversary. It is not surprising that many slip totally away from any hope of victory and leave the church attempting to find another form of peace.

It has been my experience that to attempt to live the Christian life in my own strength is useless. Knowing this as fact, one then must ask by whose power are Christians to live? This is where the third Person of the Trinity comes into our lives—the Holy Spirit—Comforter, Convicter, Teacher, Counselor. In His role as Counselor, he supplies power for the living to all believers, making the disciplined and fruitful Christian life possible. The absence of the Holy Spirit makes living the Christian life frustrating, confusing, and hopelessly difficult!

But ye are not in the flesh, but in the Spirit, if so be that the Spirit of God dwell in you. Anyone who does not have the Spirit of Christ does not belong to him (Rom. 8:9, RSV).

To live by the power of the Holy Spirit is an adventure that cannot be matched on this earth. If every believer could realize that His awesome power is waiting to be claimed, we could turn the world upside down! The problem and the fact remains that too many Christians are complacent and content just where they are. They have no desire to make an impact on this sinful world. They have no desire to win others to Jesus Christ. They have no desire to live victoriously. Therefore, they have never sought the power necessary to do these things.

If we only do the things we are comfortable doing, we do not need the power of the Holy Spirit. The power of the Spirit works in the realm of impossibility. The ordinary situations of life we can handle on our own. For the impossible, we must have the power of God's Spirit.

I want my life to count for the Kingdom. I desire to accomplish things that will have eternal significance. Nothing means more to me. In order for me to accomplish these things, **I must** have the power of the Holy Spirit supplied on a daily basis. He makes it possible for me to witness effectively to others; to put God's will before my selfish one; to live my life in obedience to Him; to rise above difficult circumstances; to uproot fear, impatience, and bitterness from my mind; to know, beyond a doubt, that Jesus Christ is the answer for a troubled world and to believe it to the extent that I am willing to give my life sharing that knowledge with others. I am challenged beyond my capabilities. My goals exceed my grasp. But I have His promise followed by His gifts:

Ye shall receive power, after that the Holy Ghost is come
upon you (Acts 1:8).

But when the Holy Spirit controls our lives he will produce
this kind of fruit in us: love, joy, peace, patience, kindness,
goodness, faithfulness, gentleness and self-control (Gal.
5:22, TLB).

# Chapter 12

# The Witness

There is an old legend which tells of the angel Gabriel greeting Jesus on His return to heaven after the resurrection. The angel inquired about plans for carrying on Christ's work on earth.

"I have left my work in the hands of my friends," Jesus answered.

"But surely you established an organization," insisted the angel.

"No, none."

"Ah, you wrote a book."

"No, I wrote no book."

"But suppose your friends fail," persisted Gabriel, "What other plans have you?"

"I have no other plan," the Master softly replied.

No other plan! He is depending solely on you and me to spread the word. Witnessing is what we **do** with what we **know** about Christ.

A unique lady graces our community with her deep and abiding love for Christ. Margaret Howard owns and manages The Miracle Book Room, the only religious bookstore in the neighboring town of Richmond. One day while visiting with her, she said to me, "Cyvette, you are Jesus to somebody." It took awhile for that statement to sink in. But the truth is that we are His hands, His feet, His lips, His heart—to someone. We are as close as some people will ever get to the love of Christ.

In a sermon by D. L. Moody, the story is told of a family torn apart by yellow fever. First, the father contracted the disease and died. Then the mother became ill. Yellow fever was so highly contagious that no one dared enter the house of those who had it except to collect a body and bury it. The young mother had a small son and, realizing that she was dying, she tried to prepare and encourage him, knowing that he would be hopelessly shunned until fear of the disease had passed. So, she called the little fellow to her bedside, and said, "My son, I am going to leave you, but when I am gone, Jesus will come to you."

Moody related that the mother died, her body was carried away, and the small boy was left alone. Although the neighbors wanted to help and comfort him, they were fearful of the pestilence. One day the boy wandered to the place where they had laid his mother, sat down on the grave, and wept himself to sleep. The next morning he awoke, alone and hungry. Soon, a stranger came along. Seeing the small boy sitting on the grave, he asked who he was waiting for. The boy remembered what his mother had told him and replied, "I am waiting for Jesus." The boy's tragic story touched the man deeply. He knelt beside the child and said, "Jesus has sent me." With a weary sigh, the boy said, "You have been so long in coming."

How long will we make those wait who need to hear the soul-saving words of comfort that Christians can offer?

As I see it, there are three ways to witness. The living witness is by far the most difficult, yet the most rewarding. No words are required—that sounds easy enough. The hard part comes in **being.** Being a living witness requires a large measure of the Holy Spirit. Human beings could not possibly live a consistent Christian life without His power.

> And so, dear brothers, I plead with you to give your bodies to God. Let them be a living sacrifice, holy—the kind he can accept (Rom. 12:1, TLB).

Several Christmases ago, our family decided to do something special to show our love for Jesus. So, Gene, the boys, and I sat down to discuss what we might do. We planned to make a giant birthday card. Gene's job was to print the letters on large squares of poster board. I would help the kids cover the letters with glue and sprinkle them with glitter. We wrote HAPPY BIRTHDAY JESUS! When we were finished, we took the squares outside, assembled our "card" across the front of the house under the Christmas lights, and stood back to admire our gift to Jesus. Catching the glow of the colored lights, the letters sparkled and twinkled our message to the entire neighborhood. Hey, everybody, this is what Christmas is all about! This is what **we** are all about—we belong to the Christ of Christmas.

Another demonstration of "living" our witness took place this winter. One crystal clear morning we awakened to a marshmallow world. The fresh snow clung to the evergreens like powdered sugar icing. The bare trees formed silhouettes against the blue sky, in silent testimony to their promised resurrection in the spring. When the sun came out, the whiteness was breathtakingly brilliant. I hated to think that soon there would be tracks in the snow, spoiling its untouched purity.

In church that morning, Gene announced a sledding party on Adam's Hill, the highest and most popular hill in Paint Lick.

The afternoon was glorious. Everywhere were the sights and sounds of happy people. Sledders bundled snugly with mufflers streaming, bright red cheeks and noses, peals of silver laughter, snowball fights, daring rides in sleds and inner tubes. And then when the merriment subsided and everyone was happily exhausted, we snuggled by the fireside at Joe Brown's house, drinking mugs of steaming hot chocolate and reliving our perfect day.

How was such a day possible? Because of Jesus Christ! We were the family of God sharing our common bond. To those who saw us, it was a "living" testimony of unity in our Savior. Word has a way of spreading in this small community, and it will be known that the people of Paint Lick United Methodist Church share their lives—happy times and sad—because Jesus lives!

As a non-Christian, I could never have had so many friends. Petty differences or jealousies always got in the way. Now I belong to a group that lives in harmony, not because we are special people, but because we serve a Savior who is!

Someone once said, "What you are speaks so loudly that I can't hear what you're saying." There is no need "telling" someone you have found the answer if you are not living it yourself. You **can** tell a book by its cover and people often read what we are before we ever open our mouths! If our living witness is valid, then we can move into a more verbal witness as the opportunities arise.

> Quietly trust yourself to Christ your Lord and if anybody asks why you believe as you do, be ready to tell him, and do it in a gentle and respectful way (1 Pet. 3:15, TLB).

The "sharing" witness may develop over a period of time. It involves cultivating the friendship of those around us in order to share Christ. Sharing is done in a casual, friendly manner with no pressure for a response.

At a Christmas party given by Gene's company some years ago, we found it perfectly natural to fit Christ into the conversation. As coworkers related their personal experiences, we told of incidents that always seemed to revolve around our relationship with Christ. No one was offended. We didn't put anyone on the spot by "don't you agree?" statements. We simply shared our life-style just as naturally as they shared theirs.

The door-knocking type of witnessing differs from the other two in that you set out to share the gospel with the purpose of leading a person to make a decision for Christ. It is a deliberate action, preceded by prayer and preparation.

I'll never forget the first time I tried this kind of witnessing. I was so unfamiliar with the Bible that I could not find **one** scripture to support what I was saying. The people I was visiting wanted to read the plan of salvation in the Bible for themselves— something besides John 3:16, that is! It was indeed an embarrassing moment, but it taught me a valuable lesson. We cannot always share what we "feel" and expect that to suffice. We must study the Word; and when we speak, it is not by our own authority, but by the authority of God Himself.

It takes a great deal of courage to witness in this way. It requires stepping out on faith, knowing the Holy Spirit has prepared the way.

A good example of this type of witnessing is the "I Found It" campaign that recently swept America. I worked on the phone, calling specific persons, giving my personal testimony, and explaining what it means to be a Christian.

Working on those phone lines with a room full of team members was inspiring! It gave me a small glimpse of the comaraderie the disciples must have experienced as they boldly proclaimed God's Word. They, too, must have often felt threatened and afraid, causing them to lean more heavily on the Savior!

We may not agree as to how to witness. Certainly, the three methods mentioned will often overlap. But we can be open to opportunities as they arise. Where there is a desire, the way will be provided. Then when the opportunity arises, we simply leave the outcome in His hands!

> In the same way there is joy in the presence of the angels of God when one sinner repents (Luke 15:10, TLB).

The joy that comes from sharing the gospel is unmatched by any other Christian experience. I can't imagine keeping anything so wonderful to myself!

# Chapter 13

# The Reward

Our journey has led us through treacherous territory—fear, impatience, selfishness, doubt, circumstances, disobedience—all common pitfalls for the Christian. Each problem has its own built-in solution and reward. In each case the solution is commitment—the reward is infinite joy. By trusting ourselves totally to the risen Savior, we can defeat the joy robbers. This is His promise:

> And whatsoever we ask, we receive of him, because we keep his commandments, and do those things that are pleasing in his sight (1 John 3:22).

If we are not totally committed to Jesus Christ, we will not even think to turn to Him with our problems and needs. With commitment to Christ, nothing is impossible. The inner joy that accompanies a Christ-centered life can be realized in any life situation.

A perfect example of the kind of total commitment of which I am speaking is powerfully portrayed in the following story.

After a banquet at our church, the guest soloist and her husband, June and Pete Peterson, remained to talk about the death of their son, Mark. Many times during the conversation we found ourselves in tears. But June and Pete had already shed their tears and now they were sharing their triumph and their joy.

It all began the winter Mark was ten years old—a winter so severe that going outdoors to play was out of the question. Since Mark enjoyed building models, he closed himself in his room to pursue his hobby. Little did the Petersons know that during that time Mark was ingesting toxic fumes from the model glue he was using.

When June noticed that Mark was looking extremely pale, she took him to the family doctor. He diagnosed the illness as a depression of the bone marrow caused by the toxic fumes. With proper treatment, Mark would recover completely. Naturally, instructions were followed to the letter, but there was no improvement. Further tests now revealed that Mark had developed leukemia. The prognosis for recovery was poor.

But Mark did not despair. He had been reared by parents who believed in the power of God to accomplish the impossible. Mark believed God would heal him.

Two-and-one-half years of suffering lay ahead for Mark before his death. Every available experimental drug was used, but with no permanent improvement. Mark suffered terribly from the drugs, but only once during the long ordeal did he complain. Often, he was so weak he could sit up for only fifteen minutes at a time. He used those minutes to do his homework so that he could keep up with his classmates. Mark was determined he would enter the eighth grade on schedule!

During the last six months of his life, Mark was given a drug called predisone, a cousin of cortisone.

It is a deadly drug which destroys the platelets in the blood. Lacking these, the blood fails to clot and hemorrhaging is always a very real danger. The drug also caused swelling and varicose veins all over Mark's body.

The final two weeks were unbearably painful. One Sunday after June had sung at a church near the hospital, she returned to Mark's room. He greeted her excitedly with the news that he had spoken with a Catholic priest. After visiting Mark's roommate, the priest had walked over to Mark's bed, stared at him sternly and asked, "Young man, are you a member of our faith?" Mark returned his gaze and replied firmly, "No, sir. I'm a born again believer." Without another word, the priest quickly departed. June asked Mark what he would have said if the priest had asked him to explain his answer. Mark replied, "I would have told him that I believe in Jesus Christ as my Savior and when I die I'm going to heaven to be with Him." Those words of assurance concerning eternal life were to be a great comfort to June and Pete in the days to come.

Mark spent the last week of his life at a Boston Children's Clinic on the eighth floor, reserved for children with terminal cancer. On Monday, the doctors decided to perform a spinal tap. Unaware of the seriousness of Mark's condition, they used a large needle to draw the fluid from the base of his spine. Within a half hour after the procedure, Mark began to experience paralysis of his lower limbs, accompanied by excruciating pain at the site of the puncture. For the first time since becoming ill, Mark openly wept. June and Pete said that many times bone marrow had been drawn from Mark's breastbone without anesthesia and, though tears would roll down his face, he did not cry out. Now he did.

Upon examination it was discovered that the needle used was too large for such a small body that was no longer producing platelets. The procedure had started the hemorrhaging. Now a large clot had formed on the spine causing the pain and paralysis. From that point on, Mark was given morphine to relieve the pain.

Not long after being put on morphine, Mark's report card arrived. It was filled with excellent marks earned under unbelievably difficult circumstances. June tried to communicate this good news to her son, but it was impossible to break through to his conscious mind.

That Friday, after a horrible week of suffering, Mark experienced a massive hemorrhage from the nose, losing literally pints of blood. He was being suctioned constantly so that he could breathe. His body was a mass of broken veins as his blood system continued to fail.

On Sunday, after having prayed by Mark's bedside for hours, June asked God to end his suffering. She left his room and paced the corridors, repeating scripture verses to keep her sanity. Exhausted, in mind and body, she went to rest in the room provided for parents of dying children. It was a room she had hoped she would never have to enter. Now her son was dying and there was nothing anyone could do.

Sometime during the night Pete came to tell her that Mark could not live much longer. Though June had been strong for over two years, now she began to shake violently. It took her over an hour to calm herself enough to dress. During that time, the doctors said Mark sat up in bed as if completely normal and casually conversed with the doctors. He reminded them all that thousands of people were praying for him. Then he slipped into semiconsciousness.

As June approached Mark's room, his screams of agony met her in the corridor. His bed was surrounded by doctors and nurses, trying to contain him. June, horrified at what she saw, ran to her son and pulled him close to her, "Mark, it's Mom. Can you hear me? It's Mom!" Mark grabbed her and held on for dear life. His face was so swollen he could no longer open his eyes, but he could hear his mother's voice.

"Would the family wish to use life support systems?" probed the doctors gently.

Pete turned to them with a grief-stricken face, "Is there any hope at all?"

Their solemn nods told him what he needed to know.

"Then let him go. We know where he's going."

Pete and June stood by, trying to comfort their suffering son. Finally, Pete put his mouth right next to Mark's ear, "Son, can you hear me? This is Dad. Mark, in just a few minutes you are going to be with Jesus. Do you understand?" Mark nodded yes. Moments passed and now Mark was gasping for air, as the body fluids crushed his lungs. Again, Pete bent over his son, "Mark, do you see Jesus coming for you?" With a last burst of strength, Mark lifted his upper body off the bed and with all his remaining might nodded yes, yes! He then took his last breath and died. June and Pete held his hands and committed his spirit unto God.

Not long after his death, the Petersons received a letter from a minister friend. It read, "Mark always said Jesus would make him well. Now He has."

> Weeping may go on all night, but in the morning there is joy (Ps. 30:5, TLB).

How does one live through such an experience, much less gain victory in it? I shared this story because there is a beautiful lesson here—not a lesson about dying, but one of life and hope. Mark's story is not unlike a story in the New Testament. Stephen was stoned to death for his belief in Jesus Christ. Though he died an agonizing death, he was faithful to his commitment to the very last breath.

Commitment is **consciously deciding** that we will put ourselves under the care and charge of Jesus Christ. If we commit ourselves to the degree that when the going gets rough, we do not question or quit, we will grow stronger through the trial.

But commitment is only the beginning. Along with the commitment comes hard work and self-discipline. It is then that we wonder if we have made the right decision.

Martin Luther's religion of "duty" failed him, even though he tried in every way to fulfill that duty. It wasn't until Luther allowed Christ to move to the center of his being, that Luther's ministry took on new power and effectiveness. John Wesley had a similar experience. His religion was a burden and a frustration to him until that glorious night he let Christ take over. At that moment, John Wesley became a new man with a new power.

Commitment is making a covenant with God to live by His Word and not by our emotions. When we have developed a commitment like that, joy and peace will be ours. Let the problems come— God is able!

> And God is able to make all grace abound toward you; that ye, always having all sufficiency in all things, may abound to every good work (2 Cor. 9:8).

Some years ago our family attended a ball game, leaving the park just as the last rays of sunlight disappeared over the horizon. All of us were shivering as the cool breeze penetrated our light summer clothing. Our youngest son, then three, ran to the car in search of warmth. As I jumped in beside him, he scampered into my lap, snuggling close. I held as much of him as I could, but it didn't satisfy him. He said, "No, Mama, like this—like this." He lifted his arms high, showing me how to grab more of him. Again I tried to cover all of the wiggly little body, but no matter what I did, there remained an unprotected arm or leg. Finally, he latched on with both arms, pulling himself next to me. I wrapped my arms tightly about him. It worked! He felt warm and secure as we held on to each other.

It is the same with our relationship to God. Though He holds and upholds, real security comes when we are holding on too! In childlike faith, we can approach our Father and seek His help in all that we do. Instead of being fearful, we can say, "Lord, deal with my fear." Instead of doubting, we can say, "Lord, help me to believe." Instead of succumbing to circumstances, we can say, "Lord, give me the power to be obedient." He will supply the power if we submit our wills to Him.

# Chapter 14

# The Joy-Maker

Not long ago, my sons begged me to go adventuring with them. For many months I had been hearing exciting stories about Chipmunk Hill. This was to be the day I would see these wonders for myself. As the ground was still lightly dusted with snow, we put on layers of warm clothing and headed for the hill.

As a matter of expedience, I suggested we drive the truck to the bridge and walk from there. I quickly got a "you've got to be kidding" look from the boys. It was obvious to them I did not yet understand what this adventure was all about!

We struck out across the hills on foot. We must have climbed fifty barbed wire fences. Along the way, we were joined by Pancake and Toby, two local dogs who find little boys irresistible. We walked for miles before we reached Paint Lick Creek. The boys had assured me that we could cross the creek by jumping from stone to stone and save ourselves quite a long hike down the back road. They hadn't figured on the melting snow which had caused the water to rise. There wasn't a stone in sight.

On the trek back to the bridge, there were three sheepish little boys, two panting dogs, and one mad mother! Not only had I been pulling Bobby John along, but helping the whining dogs over all the fences. Unaccustomed as I was to this much fresh air and exercise, my legs were aching and I was gasping for breath.

"How much farther, boys?" I panted.

They pointed in the direction from which we had just come, explaining that had we been able to cross the creek, we would be there now. At that point, I put my motherly foot down, and told them I was not going to hike another step. They begged and pleaded, but I was not going to budge.

With pointed finger, I ordered the boys home! They hung their heads dejectedly. Being the leaders for a change as Mom struggled to keep up was an exhilarating new experience for them. I could see the defeat and disappointment in their eyes. Like any mother, I began to weaken.

"Boys, how far did you say it was?"

Their faces brightened. "Only across those two fields, Mama. Come on, Mama, you can make it. It's so much fun. We might see all kinds of wild animals and there are **just three more fences to climb!"**

With no small measure of sarcasm, I replied, "Terrific!" and we trudged ahead. On the way we saw two rabbits, flushed a covey of quail, and nearly stepped on a skunk! It occurred to me that perhaps I was not seeing this adventure through their eyes. All I could think of was my aching body. I had not yet caught the boys' vision of high adventure.

But we made it to Chipmunk Hill. It was everything they had said it would be. The hill jutted steeply skyward with rocks artfully sprinkled like stepping stones. We stood in a meadow, overshadowed by huge trees that bordered the rushing creek, swollen by the melting snow. Surely heaven must be something like Chipmunk Hill! I wouldn't trade that experience for anything in the world. To think I was almost robbed of the joy because I couldn't see the vision.

The children almost missed it too. When we were making our plans to move to Kentucky, the boys threw a fit. "Oh, no!" they moaned "We can't leave our friends. We can't give up our fishing pond. Please don't make us go!"

Gene and I assured them that God never takes something away without replacing it with something better. It wasn't long after settling into their new home before the boys realized that Paint Lick, Kentucky, is little boys' paradise! They traded one small, polluted pond for many sparkling clear, see-your-face ponds! They made friends with two little boys their own ages within walking distance, who lived in adjoining farmhouses. There were woods to explore and hills to climb, and high adventure with every sunrise. There was Scraper, a dear old-new friend, to take them fishing and camping, and to captivate them with his tall tales. Patient as a saint, he always has time for his "bo-o-oys." (Starting in a low key, he sings the sound, ending an octave higher.) Then there's Mama "B," the grandmother-by-proxy, who never forgets birthdays and other special days with unexpected treats and her own brand of homemade love. Now, when we want to go home on vacation, the boys want to stay in Paint Lick!

And so it is in our walk with Christ—the great Joy-Maker. If we continually resist the call to adventurous living in Him, we will fall easy prey to the joy robbers who wait in ambush. If we are willing to climb some fences, ford some creeks, and cross some bridges, we will ultimately find ourselves in the paradise prepared for those who belong to Him.

When we meet Him face to face, I hope He can say,

> Well done, thou good and faithful servant: thou hast been faithful over a few things, I will make thee ruler over many things: enter thou into the joy of thy Lord (Matt. 25:21).